T0330016

Earth Economics

That's one small step for (a) man; one giant leap for mankind

Neil Armstrong Apollo 11 Lunar Surface Journal at
http://history.nasa.gov/alsj/a11/a11.step.html#1092413

Earth Economics

An Introduction to Demand Management, Long-Run Growth and Global Economic Governance

Peter A.G. van Bergeijk

Professor of International Economics and Macroeconomics, international Institute of Social Studies of Erasmus University, The Hague, The Netherlands, Earth

Edward Elgar
Cheltenham, UK • Northampton, MA, USA

Published by
Edward Elgar Publishing Limited
The Lypiatts
15 Lansdown Road
Cheltenham
Glos GL50 2JA
UK

Edward Elgar Publishing, Inc.
William Pratt House
9 Dewey Court
Northampton
Massachusetts 01060
USA

A catalogue record for this book
is available from the British Library

Library of Congress Control Number: 2012954983

This book is available electronically in the ElgarOnline.com
Economics Subject Collection, E-ISBN 978 1 78254 086 1

ISBN 978 0 85793 932 6 (cased)

Printed by MPG PRINTGROUP, UK

Contents

PART II   LONG RUN

PART III   EARTH GOVERNANCE AND GLOBAL PUBLIC GOODS

Figures, Diagrams and Tables

FIGURES

DIAGRAMS

TABLES

Preface

When I cleaned up the attic, I discovered something that I had forgotten. As a boy, I used to write down my address on schoolbooks and magazines as

Name: Peter van Bergeijk
Road: Warande 14
Town: Heerjansdam
Country: Holland
Planet: Earth

Somehow I lost this perspective when I grew up, only to recover it some four decades later when I was a member of the Bureau of the OECD's Economic Policy Committee's Working Party No. 1 on Macroeconomic and Structural Policy Analysis and to my frustration found out that the countries that were absolutely vital to solve the problem of global warming could not be formally engaged in the deliberations. I quit my job and became professor.

Earth Economics grew out of my teaching of open macroeconomics courses to MA students at the international Institute of Social Studies of Erasmus University, one of Europe's major development studies institutes. This book solves one of my problems. ISS students come from all countries around the globe and the level and quality of education is very heterogeneous, to say the least. Many of my students have worked after university and need a refresher. Giving an effective course in advanced macroeconomics is impossible with this kind of heterogeneity and therefore something needs to be done to get the students at the same starting level. (Incidentally, this is not a specific problem for ISS, but of all universities that have students from a great many countries with differing educational systems and levels of development as I learned when I was teaching monetary policy at Zürich university at the turn of the millennium.) For this reason I teach a crash course of basic macroeconomic principles at the beginning of the first semester at ISS in order to remedy deficient or absent knowledge. The purpose of the lecture notes on which this book is based is to close the knowledge gaps and for this reason the notes are useful both as an instruction text at the BA level and as a source for self-study. I try to explain everything that may have gone unnoticed or unexplained, from index numbers to elasticities and from equilibrium concepts to exponential growth.

In a remedial course the closed economy abstraction is an extremely useful concept because it keeps things simple so that basic concepts can be discussed without too many complicating factors. For this reason all introductory courses and textbooks in macroeconomics and economic growth start with the closed economy. These discussions are abstract, boring and without reference to the real world. This is very demotivating for students and lecturers. The reason for this unsatisfactory topic in economics 101 is that no country exists with a closed economy so that no real world examples can be given. This book changes that and uses the closed economy that all my students know so well: Earth. It is very helpful that they can all relate to a place that they inhabit and because they are from so many nations, Earth is the only common meeting ground. Importantly, by studying the economics of Earth I can provide concrete examples from the start and, as will become clear, all key concepts can be illustrated by concrete data at the world level. The decisive benefit of studying Earth, however, is that (economic) policy issues can be introduced as soon as the relevant concepts have been discussed (in the usual textbook this has to wait until theory has been sufficiently developed to incorporate interactions with other countries). And actually, that is what is going to happen in this book. I invite you to study the closed economy in a real world and policy relevant context and learn a lot about macroeconomics and Earth at the same time.

Obviously, it is from an economic theoretic point of view important to realize that we can and actually should use the closed economy model to teach and understand economic developments at the world level: unlike many economists think, closed economy models do not only serve a didactic purpose, but actually make sense empirically. This is a nice point, but that is not the only goal that I want to achieve with this book. By teaching eartheconomics I frame the major issues in (economic) policy in a context that goes beyond nations, nationalities and nationalism. I want students to become earthlings.

Earth, December 12, 2012

Acknowledgements

During the years 2010 – 2012 many students of the ISS Course 9150 asked questions that helped to (re)focus the manuscript. This book would not have existed without their input.

Sameer Khatiwada and Verónica Escudero guided me through the ILO statistics; Figure 6.1 is based on the underlying data of the ILO's 2012 *World of Work* report and were kindly provided by the Institute for Labour Studies. Figure 6.3 appears by permission of Chris Elvidge and co-authors. Figure 11.3 appears by permission of the International Competition Network. Alex Dreher supplied the data of the world data for the KOF index of globalization reported in Figure 13.2.

The manuscript benefitted from detailed comments by Djalita Fialho, Jan van Heemst, Rolph van der Hoeven, Wil Hout and Howard Nicholas. The analyses in Part III were presented during the early autumn of 2012 at seminars at the universities of Antwerp (12 September) and Groningen (19 October) and these discussions helped me to clarify my thinking on the economics of the provision of global public goods. Ward Warmerdam and Victoria Litherland provided useful editorial services.

1. Introduction: It is the Only One We Have

This is definitely not a mainstream macroeconomics textbook. *Earth Economics* studies the economy of our planet from the perspective of an autarkic system (a 'closed economy'). Macroeconomics is essentially national in orientation as it deals with national policies (admittedly often in an international context). Eartheconomics focuses on the global level. It does so by ignoring the constituent national and regional parts of the planet economy and thus we will focus on policy making that increases global rather than national welfare. Indeed, eartheconomics is a subject on its own. Economists analyse world issues by aggregating nations into regions and regions into even larger entities. Starting at a low level of aggregation (the nation state), they expect to arrive at the top (the world economy), but it is more probable that they actually lose sight of the whole.

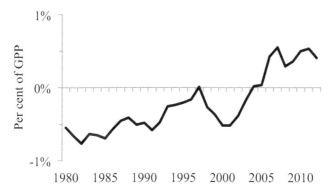

Source: IMF World Economic Outlook April 2012 Database

Figure 1.1 Aggregate of all national current accounts according to IMF

Figure 1.1 illustrates the error of aggregation by means of the total of the current accounts of all nations. The current account measures the external financial flows (international payments and receipts) of a country and since a payment of one country is always a receipt for another country, the sum of those flows should be zero. Figure 1.1 shows that this logical condition is not met in the major analytical database of the International Monetary Fund. It is clear that before 2005 the national data collectively must have overestimated the payments of countries (as the total of all national current accounts is negative) or, what amounts to the same, underestimated receipts. Since 2005 the total of all current accounts is positive and the national current accounts therefore must on average overestimate the net receipts (that is: receipts minus payments) of the countries of the world. Figure 1.1 therefore clearly shows that the underlying national and regional data in the IMF's flagship publication, the *World Economic Outlook* must be wrong on average and that the direction of error differs between the pre-crisis period and the period of the Great Recession. By implication the analyses built on these data must be biased. Incidentally, this is the last time that we will take a look at the global current account: eartheconomics is based on the recognition that Earth's current account should be zero until Earth starts to trade with other planets.

Indeed, the idea of the whole – the global economy – is often lost in the analyses of the international organizations. Commenting on this phenomenon, Robert Wade, a leading development economist at the London School of Economics, notes that:

> The World Bank and the IMF still buy into this basic idea. They pay remarkably little attention to the global economy, instead taking the country as the unit and seeing the world economy as an aggregate of countries. The whole thirty-year run of the World Bank's flagship, *The World Development Report*, takes the country as the unit of observation and prescription, and says very little about the international system in which countries have to operate. The recent push away from macroeconomics towards thinking small reinforces the same tendency (Izurieta 2009, p. 1162).

Eartheconomics starts at the highest level of aggregation offering a new approach to world economic issues. Macroeconomics, so to say, studies the bees, eartheconomics studies the beehive.

The methods of macroeconomics and eartheconomics, however, only differ in degree and are not fundamentally different (as is the case with microeconomics that studies the behaviour of the *individual* firm, consumer, employee, etc.). Both macroeconomists and eartheconomists study collectives (the consumers, the firms, the unemployed, government, etc.) and typically are interested in output, (un)employment, inflation, wages and income, interest rates, government spending and taxation. But macroeconomists do this at the level of nations and thus have to explicitly consider the economic interactions with other nations (trade, foreign investment, lending, borrowing, development aid and remittances) that are registered on the Balance of Payments, and also have to study the movement of exchange rates. From this perspective an eartheconomist has an easier life: Earth does not interact economically with other planets (yet).

1.1 AN INTRODUCTION TO BASIC CONCEPTS

Earth Economics provides a sound and accessible introduction of basic macroeconomic concepts, including methods and principles, and their application to real world data. I use the latest statistical material and guide the reader to relevant sources on Earth statistics including production, (un)employment, population, the components of effective demand, income distribution, the world capital stock (including natural resources), etc. All macroeconomic concepts will thus be introduced using real world data which will both enable a better understanding of the concepts and provide the reader with up to date knowledge of the factual state of the world economy.

This book respects the heritages of Keynes (short-term demand management: the ISLM model) and Solow (long-run neoclassical growth). I do so not out of economic respect, but because these tools are very useful to understand the Great Recession and also because they are in a down to earth manner elementary to analyse the policy responses to that crisis. If you are most interested in maths, micro foundations and the latest complexities of modern macroeconomic theory, or if you want to learn only about your own home country, then my advice is to put this book aside. But before you leave, consider Text Box 1.1 that lists recent top notch references that use the basic tools of macroeconomics that feature in *Earth Economics* as well.

Text Box 1.1 References on ISLM, neoclassical growth and growth accounting

Colander (2004) provides a review of trends in the use of the ISLM model since the early 1970s noting that empirical research with the model was absent before 1980 but substantially revived after 1980.

King (2000) provides a closed economy introduction to new versions of the ISLM model that take (rational) expectations and optimization into account.

Mankiw, Romer and Weil (1992) estimated the Solow growth model; this article runs in the ten thousand quotations and continues to inspire a lot of research.

Kumar and Russell (2002) do a thorough analysis of production frontiers and a growth accounting decomposition.

Although the limitations of the ISLM model and the basic Solow growth model are well recognized by their users, the models still serve a number of useful purposes. In particular in policy discussions these models often provide the common framework to which one can refer during discussions and, moreover, these models are often used to communicate a more complicated underlying analysis. The ISLM model essentially explains how interest rates and production are influenced by shocks and, moreover, what policy can and cannot do. A lot of new features have been introduced in the model including an aggregate production function, a labour market and debt dynamics that add complications that are relevant in the real world. These complicating factors are important for a good understanding of how Earth's economy works and what recent macroeconomic discussions are all about. The Solow model essentially explains how saving, investment, population growth and technology interact in the long run to determine productivity, that is: economic welfare. Versions of this standard neoclassical growth model interestingly provide useful insights into poverty traps and the requirements of a take-off towards sustained growth. Sometimes policy advice derived from these models is contradictory providing the useful lesson that policies that are good for the long run may not be applicable, useful or warranted over the short term (and *vice versa* of course).

Earth Economics stops where other textbooks start to develop links and interactions with other countries or other important add-ons like (rational) expectations and micro foundations. Some have asked me why on earth I stop when things get interesting. I have two simple answers to that challenge. Firstly, Earth data are not yet sufficiently available to allow more complicated theories to be meaningfully illustrated and, secondly and more importantly, it *is* interesting to stop and analyse our current state of affairs from the perspective of the closed economy that Earth ultimately is. Eartheconomists study short-term fluctuations and long-run growth in the Earth economy. They use this highly aggregated level of analysis because the world economy is the only economy where the concept of a closed economy – one that does not trade with other economies – makes sense. After all Earth does not trade (yet) with Moon or Mars. Of course the application of this concept to real economic activities does not mean that there is no international trade on Earth. (I also note for fun that the necessary economic theories are available once interplanetary trade becomes a reality in the future; see, for example, Krugman 1978 and Hickman 2008.) The countries of our world trade with each other; my point is simply that our world does not trade with other worlds and in this sense the application of the closed economy concept is the only logically appropriate one. The Earth perspective often provides a different and more challenging picture than the usual analyses based on aggregate or average findings for the individual countries in the world economy. The Earth perspective shows the big picture and asks nagging questions: What would be the best course of action for a world government? How could we improve well-being of the earthling? By stopping short of the topical issues in open macroeconomics these key questions for humanity emerge in a framework that critically challenges many of the mainstream policy analyses and recipes.

1.2   FROM MACRO TO EARTH

Macroeconomics deals with the performance, structure, behaviour and decision-making of an entire economy. Typically, the analysis takes place at the national level, and macroeconomists study how production, (un)employment, and prices interact. One important tool is the development of theoretical models that explain the relationships between income, production, consumption, unemployment, inflation, savings and investment. These models can be constructed in many ways: in graphs, diagrams and mathematical equations. In this book you will learn to appreciate the merits and weaknesses of each of the different ways to express how macroeconomic variables relate to one another.

Eartheconomics is no *l'art pour l'art*. The questions that we study are relevant as economic policies influence large numbers of people around the globe in a very concrete way: unemployment, growth and inflation influence our daily lives. The important issues are to understand:

- the causes and consequences of short-run fluctuations (the business cycle),
- the determinants of long-run economic growth (increases in national income) and the long economic waves, and
- what we can and, equally importantly, cannot do to stimulate development and prevent or remedy downturns of the economy.

Answering the last question (what we can and cannot do) always requires a close examination of actual economic variables, their development and relations with other economic variables. This is why *Earth Economics* is as much about theory and empirical research as it is about policy.

The key abstraction of *Earth Economics* comes at some costs. Firstly, this perspective 'neglects' that countries can learn from, cooperate with and help each other, but also that countries differ to a large extent, focus on national interests and may, for example, not agree on the appropriateness of some considered economic, monetary and/or financial policy. Secondly, the construction of Earth data is often complicated especially when statistical procedures differ largely between countries, when statistically important countries do not collect the data, or when political correctness and ideology plays a role (in the former Communist countries unemployment officially did not exist so it was set at zero). These costs should not be neglected, but they should also not be exaggerated and – importantly – be balanced against the benefits of a new manner of framing policy questions that are important for world development.

Text Box 1.2 Earth data

You need to do some economic detective work to find the economic data for planet Earth, because there is no Planetary Bureau of Statistics to which you can turn. Relatively reliable data are available for Gross Domestic Product (both nominal, at constant prices and at purchasing power parity), consumption, investment, government spending and inflation (Consumer Price index, GDP deflator and deflators for investment, government expenditure and consumption) and the (potential) workforce (both population and active population). These data sets that are provided by the International Monetary Fund (www.imf.org), the World Bank (www.worldbank.org), the United Nations (www.unctad.org) and the International Labour Organization (www.ilo.org) have been used in this book and will be used in the exercises so that the reader will get acquainted with the ins and outs of many international data. Sometimes the data are only available for a few years (an example is the world capital stock), are provided only once in a while (as in the case of the world output gap estimates of the IMF) or simply very incoherent and bad. For the world interest rate this book follows the convention to use a US rate. This may turn out to become an unsatisfactory choice, for example, if US debt problems were to influence US rates differently than the rates of other countries.

Sometimes the sources contradict each other yielding different estimates of growth, productivity and so on. This is a normal phenomenon (although not always reported as such). If you are interested in measurement you may wish to consult van Bergeijk (1998) or Morgenstern (1950).

1.3   PLAN OF THE BOOK

The next chapter is devoted to global National Accounting (or more precisely: Planetary Accounting) in order to introduce the most important tool that economists use to measure economic aggregates, to explain important statistical conventions and to provide a broad overview of spending and income categories at the planet level. Following this important chapter we will study eartheconomics in three different parts.

Part I is devoted to the short term and studies the fluctuations and policy responses (demand management). Chapter 3 discusses Earth's business cycle dealing with fluctuations in production, prices and unemployment. Chapter 4 provides the basic eartheconomic model that deals with consumption, investment and saving and discusses the global saving glut. Chapter 5 endogenizes investment discussing several investment theories and derives the conditions for product market equilibrium (the so-called IS curve). Chapter 6 introduces government and deals with taxation and public debt dynamics. Chapter 7 introduces money and derives money market equilibrium (the LM curve). Chapter 8 brings the elements of Chapters 4 to 7 together in order to build the eartheconomic demand schedule, to confront this with the supply side of the economy and to analyse how the world output gap develops and relates to unemployment. Chapter 9 deals with policy puzzles generating insights into why economists disagree and about what. The chapter provides in an interesting way a number of recapitulations and exercises to test the ability to use the tools of short-term analysis.

Part II focuses on the long run. Chapter 10 starts with the very long-run perspective of two millennia of growth and productivity before moving towards the Harrod-Domar and Solow models. Chapter 11 uses different versions of Solow-like models to take a look at the take off into a sustainable growth period and at impediments of growth, including poverty and middle-income traps. Chapter 12 discusses the long economic waves and the unsustainability of exponential growth (both from an economic and an ecological point of view) in order to offer an alternative perspective on the Great Recession.

Part III deals with global governance (Chapter 13 looks at the past and Chapter 14 looks at the future). In this Part we will step a bit outside the boundaries of a traditional economics textbook because there is analysis, philosophy and politics: this Part studies the developments of the *economic* conditions for the provision of global public goods (and for that it is necessary to study the amount and size of nations that make up the world community). This provides a basis to understand the prospects for policy coordination and multilateral rules and regulations. It will allow us to take a look at new forms of global governance that have emerged since the start of the millennium and at the role that the emerging economies are and will be playing in the international institutions.

1.4 HOW TO USE THIS BOOK

This is a textbook and therefore *Earth Economics* contains exercises and lists key concepts at the end of each chapter. Exercises are embedded in the main text and offer the reader moments to reflect on the arguments and methods presented. Since I believe strongly in self-study the answers to the exercises are included as an appendix to this book. I have refrained from referring to debates and studies that are essentially framed in national perspectives. The list of references at the end of this book is thus a useful starting point for the study of the economics of Earth; I maintain a dedicated website at www.eartheconomics.info where I list additions to that emerging literature.

You can use this book in four ways. The first use of the book is to learn more about the empirics of the Earth economy and about the global policy issues during the Great Recession. This is the first book with an exclusive focus on Earth and you can benefit from the collection of data from a great many sources and studies and their presentation in a consistent and comprehensive framework.

The second use of *Earth Economics* is as a textbook in a preparatory course in macroeconomics at the bachelor's level or a refresher course. The reader is alerted that the book abstracts from all open economy issues, although sometimes clear messages for policy coordination emerge.

The third use at yet another level is as an introduction to the tools and concepts that economists use to discuss economics. Non-economists should be able to understand that debate and with some effort they can learn how to survive in a discussion with economists: where to ask questions, where to listen, where to skip and where to ignore.

Or the reader can simply start in Part III on global economic governance. This part can be read without any prior knowledge and deals in a non-technical way with the economics of global public good provision in the context of the emergence of fast growing and populous countries.

1.5 KEY CONCEPTS

- Aggregate
- Autarky
- Closed economy
- Current account
- Data

- Eartheconomics
- Macroeconomics
- Microeconomics
- Net

2. Planet Accounts

One difficulty with eartheconomics is that you cannot observe eartheconomic variables directly. In a shop you can see the products in that shop and observe the amounts sold, the inventories and the prices of each item. In a factory you can count the products and observe the employees. At home you know the income of your household and your spending and saving. But you cannot see consumption, production, saving or the price level of Earth. Still, both understanding macroeconomics and policy making requires numbers. We need to know how many products are produced and bought and at what prices. Is consumption of all people going up or down? Has the purchasing power of money changed? How much are we saving? And what about Earth's investment in human and physical capital?

2.1 WHY ACCOUNTING?

The most important method to collect and present economic data at the macroeconomic level of an individual country are the National Accounts and for eartheconomics the equivalent is the Planet Accounts that we will study in this chapter. Eartheconomics would be blind without these accounts. The accounts are needed for:

- analysis (understanding the relations between variables, quantification and testing of the strength of these relationships and estimating the parameters of econometric models),
- policy (understanding and predicting the impact of policy instruments often with the use of simulation models) and
- assessment or performance measurement (*ex post* evaluation of policies or – equally relevant – the absence of policies).

Planet Accounts are for the world economy what the business accounts are for the firm. Management cannot do without such accounts because these are the basis to judge performance and to find out which activities add value and which do not. Without detailed business accounts firms will go broke.

The starting point of National Accounting is therefore the recognition that economic policy makers need reliable, systematic and consistent estimates of aggregate economic activity.

Exercise 2.1 UN National Accounts Database
- Go to the UN National Accounts Main Aggregates Database at http://unstats.un.org/unsd/snaama/.
- Select 'Data Availability' and check the status of the data for your home country.
- Select 'Data Selection' and 'Country Profile'. Next select the most recent year for which data are available for your home country and choose 'GDP by kind of Expenditure' and calculate the share of final consumption in per cent of GDP.

Three factors helped to prepare the ground for national accounting: the Great Depression of the 1930s, the Keynesian idea of economic stabilization and demand management, and war planning during the Second World War. This is not to say that no earlier attempts existed to measure and compare the total income or production of the people in a country, because we can find many such attempts in history. The point is that the systematic and regular collection and publication of such data started in the second half of the twentieth century.

Text Box 2.1 Differences between Planet Accounts and National Accounts

Planet Accounts ultimately are based on National Accounts. So the data and observations on which these two sorts of accounts rest are identical, but National Accounts explicitly distinguish between domestic and international flows and sources, whereas Planet Accounts do not distinguish final and intermediate products by country of origin. So National Accounts include exports and imports of goods and services and capital flows. Countries can run a Balance of Trade surplus or deficit which is financed by other countries. This option does not exist for Earth.

Another complicating factor is (net) foreign factor income that is paid to non-residents involved in the production of goods and services. Net foreign factor payments create a difference between National Product (the production of the non-foreign or resident factors of production) and Domestic Product (the value of goods and services created in a country) and likewise for National Income and Domestic Income. In Planet Accounting these issues do not arise.

In 1947 the United States published the first National Accounts. The United Nations set the rules of the game in 1952 when it published its manual *A System of National Accounts and Supporting Tables*. Nowadays most countries prepare National Accounts adhering to global standards codified in the System of National Accounts 2008 (you may wish to take a look at http://unstats.un.org/unsd/nationalaccount/sna2008.asp). Detailed discussions of accounting and estimation issues are provided in Bos (2009), UN (2003) and Lequiller and Blades 2006).

2.2 GETTING THE NUMBERS

The goal of Planet Accounting is not only the creation of consistent numbers and to assess the health status of the world economy but also and especially to generate knowledge about economic processes. The three issues in which we are interested in accounting are production, income and spending and these are reflected in three sets of accounts (Text Box 2.2) that are not independent: we are interested in the creation of goods and services both from the perspective of production and because production generates income.

Text Box 2.2 Accounts for production, distribution and expenditure

Production
The value of output and the goods and services that have been used in the production as inputs are registered on the production accounts. Total output minus intermediate inputs yields Gross Planet Product (GPP).

Distribution
The distribution of planetary income deals with the distribution over the so-called primary factors of production (broad categories: labour, nature, capital and entrepreneurship) as well as over sectors (enterprises, households, government) of the planetary economy. The income accounts show primary and secondary income flows. Primary income is the income generated in production (wages, rents, profits) and the redistribution of part of that income via government taxes, subsidies and social benefit payments). The bottom line is disposable income or 'Planet Income'.

Expenditure
The planetary income is either spent on current expenditures or saved. The expenditure accounts are used to register expenditures. The bottom line of the account provides total value added in the economy or Gross Planet Product.

The formulation of these three key issues and the accounts that are used for their registration already suggests that we may and will use different methods of measurement to arrive at estimates of aggregate concepts at the eartheconomic level. We can measure the goods and services produced, but we can also start from wages, rents, interest and profits (so summing the incomes of the primary factors of production) or look at expenditures. Indeed, in the accounting process three approaches play a major role: the expenditure approach (Table 2.1 provides an example), the value added approach (Table 2.2) and the income approach (Table 2.3). It is important to realize that these approaches relate essentially to the same process of value creation although they focus on different manifestations of the process. Equally important is to realize that the approaches can be used as a cross check or as a means to fill in the white accounting spots (as will be done in Exercise 2.3).

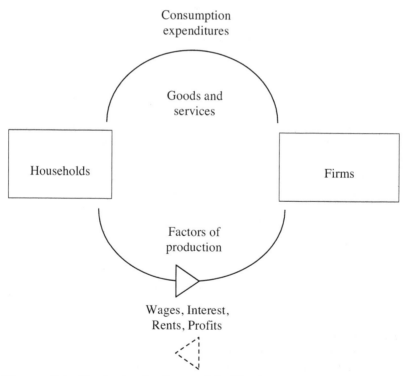

Diagram 2.1   Simple circular flow model of Earth economy

Circular Flow Model

The accounts describe the circular flows of goods, production factors and money in an economy. Diagram 2.1 illustrates that goods flow from firms to households. Households provide factors of production to the firms. Money flows in the other direction. Production generates income. Income is spent.

Diagram 2.1 provides a very simplified view on the economy of Earth. We have only two sectors: households and firms. So there is no government sector and no financial sector. Income equals the expenditures on goods and services (consumption); so there is no saving and because all goods and services are consumed no part of production is used to invest. Finally, much economic activity is going on within the sector of the firms. This activity is not homogeneous and we would like to see what happens in agriculture, in industry and in the services sector. Also most firms buy goods, materials and services from other firms (often in other branches).

So while the simple circular flow model shows some of the basic principles behind the Planetary Accounts it cannot be used to describe reality. If we want to say something meaningful about the planetary economy we will have to introduce more sectors and more spending categories.

Intermediate and Final Output

An important distinction is between intermediate output and final output. All goods and services that are used up in the production of the final product are intermediate. Examples are raw materials, components, semi-finished goods and services, that are used to finance production and to transport and distribute the products. Goods and services that are not used for further processing in the economy are final. The distinction between intermediate and final is determined by the exchange that is taking place. The paint that is sold to a general contractor is an intermediate good and becomes only final when he paints your house; but the paint bought by a consumer is final consumption. Final production in the planetary economy consists of the following items:

- Consumption, that is consumer items (goods and services bought by households for final consumption) and the output of the public services that cannot be attributed to individuals (legal system, defence, etc.).
- Investment: the rest. Goods unsold remain in inventories. Other goods are used for fixed capital formation, that is other non-consumption goods such as buildings, infrastructure, machinery and constructions. Note that changes in inventories can be positive (so the amounts of goods in stock increases) but also negative (in Table 2.1 inventories are run down).

Table 2.1 Final spending components, 2009, trillions (10^{12}) of US$, current prices

Final consumption expenditure	45.3	
Household consumption expenditure		34.7
General government final consumption expenditure		10.6
Gross capital formation	12.3	
Gross fixed capital formation		12.5
Changes in inventories		-0.2
Gross Planet Product	57.6	

Source: UN National Accounts Main Aggregates Database

It is interesting to see how the final spending components develop over time. Typically this requires that we take account of inflation (increases in prices). In the next section we will go into the details of accounting at constant prices, but in Figure 2.1 we deploy another solution as we use the shares of final spending components in Gross Planet Product (since both the nominator and denominator are in current prices, inflation does not play havoc on the comparison over time).

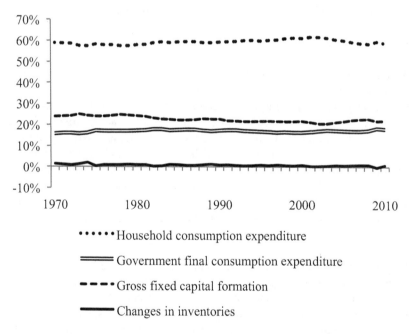

•••••Household consumption expenditure

═══ Government final consumption expenditure

━ ━ ━Gross fixed capital formation

━━━Changes in inventories

Source: See Table 2.1

Figure 2.1 Shares of final expenditure in GPP (1970 – 2010)

Table 2.2 presents the composition of Planetary Product by economic activity. The classification follows the UN's International Standard Industrial Classification (ISIC Rev. 4, see http://unstats.un.org/unsd/cr/registry/).

Table 2.2 Planetary accounts by economic activity, 2009, trillions of dollars, current prices

Agriculture, hunting, forestry, fishing (ISIC A-B)	2	4%
Mining, utilities (ISIC C-E)	3	6%
Manufacturing (ISIC D)	9	18%
Construction (ISIC F)	3	6%
Wholesale, retail trade, restaurants and hotels (ISIC G-H)	8	14%
Transport, storage and communication (ISIC I)	4	7%
Other activities (ISIC J-P)	24	46%
Total Value Added	53	100%

Source: see Table 2.1

Note: ISIC is the International Standard Industrial Classification

Note that Table 2.2 reports value added for groups of activities; that is: after subtraction of intermediate inputs, both from other industries and from the firms involved in the own activity. Value added is the contribution to the product by the specific activity. A banana produced in agriculture will be transported and move through wholesale and retail (the shop) or restaurants and hotels (if you have a banana split as dessert) to final consumption.

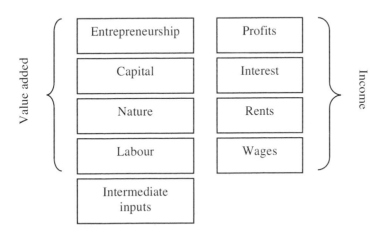

Diagram 2.2 Production, value added and income

Consider Diagram 2.2 that on the left hand side illustrates how a firm creates value. The firm uses intermediate inputs (raw materials or components produced by other firms), labour, nature (often land) and capital and realizes a price for its output that enables it to make a profit. (For some small scale units profits have a mixed income character.) It uses its turnover, first to pay for intermediate inputs, second to pay for wages, rents and interest (the so-called operational surplus) and the remainder is the reward for entrepreneurship (the latter may also be negative if the price is too low to recover costs so that the profit turns into a net loss). It is clear from Diagram 2.2 that value added by definition equals income. Basically we have thus three measures that are used in Planet Accounting in order to estimate Planet Product (PP).

- Production approach: $PP = value\ added_{industry\ 1} + value\ added_{industry\ 2} + value\ added_{industry\ 3} + ...$
- Expenditure approach: $PP = Consumption + Investment$
- Income approach: $PP = Wages + Interest + Rents + Profits$

In theory these approaches should yield the same results; in practice this never happens due to measurement errors and also because the data are collected with a great number of different methods (including surveys, tax records, censuses) that for different reasons may be inaccurate or introduce faulty or inaccurate numbers (for example, tax data may for obvious reasons understate actual income). For example, we can combine the expenditure and income approaches so that we have:

$$Consumption + Investment = PP = Wages + Interest + Rents + Profits$$

This may help to crosscheck the accounts, but also to find out what numbers apply to activities or sectors where we do not have sufficient or sufficiently good data. For example, if we do not have a good registration for rents, but reasonably reliable data for consumption, investment, wages, interest and profits, then we can use the reliable data to estimate the value of rents that would be consistent with those data. In this way the accounting framework provides a manner to integrate all these data and to work towards consistent estimates of production, income, consumption, investment, saving, etc.

The accounting often should be seen as work in progress and it is not uncommon to have several revisions of data in the years following the first estimate of domestic product. In addition to these regular updates or new estimates, substantial and official revisions occur when it is recognized that economic activity has been covered inadequately, for example, because the products were completely new and therefore went unregistered by the official statistics. Other corrections involve changes in the methodology or the registration of economic observations. Such corrections then apply to earlier years as well. Revisions occur also in economies with very sophisticated national statistical agencies and long traditions in applying standards of national accounting. Maddison (1995) discusses a number of these revisions ranging from 6 per cent of Gross Domestic Product in The Netherlands in 1969 to 25 per cent in Greece in 1990. Most revisions are upward revisions, but when new methodologies are introduced also negative revisions occur (Macao in 2008 is a recent example).

Exercise 2.2 Contribution of economic activities
- Go to UN National Accounts Main Aggregates Database at http://unstats.un.org/unsd/snaama/
- Select 'Data Selection', 'Basic Data Selection' and 'World'.
- Select 'GDP by kind of activity' and calculate the shares of manufacturing industry in Planetary Product and prepare a graph for the period 1970 – present.

The Planet Accounts can be presented in a traditional T-type account with resources, receipts and inputs on the debit side of the account and uses or expenditures on the credit side, but more often the accounts are presented in matrix format (see Diagram 2.3).

Uses or Outputs

Resources or Inputs	Intermediate Output	Final Output (Consumption, Investment) *(N.B. Total = GPP)*	Total of Intermediate and Final Outputs
	Production Factors: (Wages, Rents, Interest, Profit) *(N.B. Total = GPP)*	*(N.B. Total Inputs = Total Outputs)*	
	Total inputs		

Diagram 2.3 Planet Accounting Matrix

The obvious advantage is that the matrix can be read from left to right and from top to bottom so that the reader can observe simultaneously how resources are used, what output results, what income results and how this is spent. Inside the boxes of Diagram 2.3 we can have as many industries (both lines and columns) and final demand components as we want. Also the factors of production can be more detailed (for example high skilled and low skilled labour). The top of the accounting matrix is also known as an input output table that essentially deals with intra-industry flows (that is, intermediate production) and final demand.

2.3   SPECIFIC MEASUREMENT ISSUES

Earthlings seem to know what we mean by Planet Product and Planet Income but typically the use of that term is a bit sloppy especially in the popular press. When we discuss the developments of economic aggregates such as consumption it is important to be precise. Are we discussing the real development of consumption in which case we know that the volume (or quantity) of goods and services that consumers are buying has changed or are we discussing the nominal value of consumption. If the latter is the case inflation may play havoc, because it increases the reported nominal value (goods and services become more expensive), but that does not necessarily mean that the quantity of goods and services has increased as well. So the devil is in the detail and it is important to check which adjectives are applied to the aggregate economic concepts that are reported in the accounts.

Current Prices Versus Constant Prices

The basis of the accounting process is the registration of quantities (amounts sold, produced, consumed, in stock, etc.) and the prices of those quantities. Multiplication of price and quantity yields the values (or nominal amounts) and adding these values provides us with the value of the aggregate. We can summarize this recipe with the help of notation as $V_t = \Sigma Q_t P_t$ where V is the value, Q is the quantity and P is the price related to that quantity. The subscript t is the year to which the data refer. In this case values, prices and quantities all relate to the same year. The mathematical notation Σ says that we have to sum all the components of the aggregate.

So far all values were in current prices. Current price comparisons are appropriate if we compare values for one year, but if we want to make a comparison over time we need to take into account that the prices of the goods and services and of the factors of production change. One way to do this is to use the prices of one specific year and apply these prices to the other years. When we use the prices of one year, for example 2005 the resulting aggregates are reported as 'at constant 2005 prices'. Typically measurement of quantities and prices for the accounts takes place in the same year. Underlying each year are thus the observed prices and quantities of that year and the accounts will report these data 'at current prices'. So for each year for which we have accounts we also have prices and quantities. The trick to arrive at constant 2005 prices is to use the actual quantities for a particular year, but the prices for 2005. Invoking again the mathematical notation we can write the 2006 aggregate in 2005 prices as $V_{2006}=\Sigma Q_{2006}P_{2005}$.

Table 2.3 by way of illustration summarizes the income accounts in constant 1995 prices for the manufacturing sector. The data have been derived from the world input output project (see http://www.wiod.org/).

Table 2.3 Planet income account for manufacturing sector at constant prices (1995 dollars)

	1995		2006	
High skilled labour	0.8	13%	0.8	12%
Medium skilled labour	2.0	33%	2.1	29%
Low skilled labour	0.8	14%	1.0	14%
Total wages and salaries	3.6	59%	4.0	55%
Operating surplus	2.5	41%	3.2	45%
Total inputs	6.1	100%	7.2	100%

Source: Erumban et al. (2011)

Gross versus Net

As discussed in Section 2.2 we need to substract the intermediate inputs from output in order to arrive at the value added that constitutes the contribution of the firm or sector to the output that is generated in the economy. In addition to these visible intermediate inputs invisible inputs are important that consist of the wear and tear of fixed capital (buildings, machinery, equipment, etc.). The wear and tear of capital goods contribute to production over many years and therefore their costs have to be written off over a longer period than the single year to which the accounts apply. The amount that is written off during the reporting period is the depreciation. In addition to wear and tear, capital goods can lose value because technological developments make it economically obsolete. Even brand new fax machines are almost worthless since email provides a better and cheaper alternative. One problem with depreciation is that the clear and transparent general accounting rule (namely to estimate depreciation on the basis of the replacement value) is not followed by all enterprises. Indeed, many competing theories exist on business accounting and the decision on the reported depreciation may in addition be influenced by cash flow considerations and tax optimization. For this reason debates amongst economists most often do not consider depreciation. A macroeconomic concept is labelled 'gross' when no allowance has been made for depreciation; the label 'net' is applied after deduction of depreciation.

So we have *Net Planet Product* = *Gross Planet Product – Depreciation*, and likewise we have Net Planet Income and Net Planet Expenditure.

Market Prices versus Factor Costs

The market price in many countries includes indirect taxes (taxes that are levied on goods and services and not on factors of production). Such taxes include excise duties, value added taxes (VAT) and taxes on turnover. These taxes are paid by the final consumer, levied by the seller and ultimately collected by the tax authorities from the seller. The government may not only impose taxes; it can also provide subsidies (for example on food) that ensure that the market price is lower than the actual value added or actual factor incomes paid out of that value added. Clearly it makes a difference where we measure economic activities: in the shops and at the market valuation is at market prices, but when we measure wages, profits, rents and interest we measure eartheconomic concepts at factor costs.

So we have $PP_{market\ prices} = PP_{factor\ costs} + Indirect\ Taxes - Subsidies$ or $PP_{market\ prices} = PP_{factor\ costs} + Net\ Indirect\ Taxes$

Exercise 2.3 Construction of Planet Accounts
Construct Planet Accounts with the following information.
- The Earth economy consists of two branches/industries: Manufacturing (MANUF) and non-manufacturing (OTHER). All output can be allocated to MANUF and OTHER. There is no government sector in this economy.
- Manufacturing firms produce intermediate products both for MANUF (9) and for OTHER (13). Likewise, non-manufacturing firms provide 11 to MANUF and 1 to OTHER.
- Total inputs are 50 for MANUF and 35 for OTHER.
- Total wages in the economy are 33.
- Rents, interest and profit in MANUF are 1, 2 and 9, respectively.
- Wages, rents and interest in OTHER are 15, 3 and 4, respectively.
- Final consumption of manufactured goods is 17 and changes in inventories are 2.
- Fixed capital formation in OTHER is 4. There are no changes in inventories in OTHER.

Shadow Economy

It is important to recognize that many transactions go unregistered. This is the case for amongst others illegal transactions (including crime, drugs and prostitution), transactions that are unreported in order to avoid taxes and also when production does not take place in establishments. All these activities are located in the informal or shadow sector of the economy, That is: outside the public sector and the enterprises (the formal economy) from which the statistical offices collect their data.

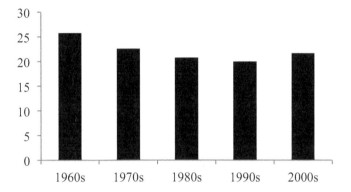

Source: Elgin and Oztunali (2012), Table 3, p. 11

Figure 2.2 Share of the shadow economy in per cent of GPP (1960s – 2000s)

At the global level informality is an issue (Figure 2.2) and despite the progress since the 1960s to bring economic activities into the formal sector of the economy, a large part of planet income (between a fifth and a quarter) is not reported in the Planet Accounts. This is especially relevant since eartheconomic conditions will have an impact on the share of the informal sector. In a downturn workers in the formal sector will become unemployed and may shift to informal labour (for example become self-employed).

Sustainability

The use of Gross Planet Product is increasingly being criticized because it only considers income generated and neglects the fact that in the end welfare is determined by Earth's assets. The depletion and destruction of natural assets only shows up in the National Accounts as a positive income stream while actually Earth and in particular next generations are becoming poorer. Likewise consumption is valued as something positive while consumption actually destroys goods. Consuming less means that the stock of assets is not depleted so that humanity could be said to become richer when it consumes less. These issues have been recognized also by economists (Boulding, 1966, is an example), but are not reflected in mainstream economics. In the same vein investment in education and knowledge adds to the human capital stock that can be used over and over again without creating a stream of income (otherwise Pythagoras' theorem could easily solve the Greek debt problem). All in all GPP covers the flow of income and not the change in the stock of assets. Both the World Bank (2011b) and the UN (2012) have therefore started projects to account global assets aimed at inclusive wealth accounting. These projects take changes in estimated stocks of assets as the basis for estimating flows. Note, however, that GPP itself is not wrong but the narrowly minded use that is often made of it. Planet Accounts continue to provide a consistent instrument to measure economic activity.

2.4 FROM DESCRIPTION TO ANALYSIS

We have paid a lot of attention to planet accounting concepts and problems because numbers, measurement and data collection are the basis for policy making and understanding. Now that we have discussed these issues we can move to the next stage. You should, however, not forget that theories and policies that do not relate to actual numbers run substantial risk of becoming silly, outdated, or simply very wrong.

2.5 KEY CONCEPTS

- Constant prices
- Consumption
- Depreciation
- Expenditure approach
- Factor costs
- Final expenditure/production
- Fixed capital formation
- Flow
- Gross
- Income approach
- Income flow model
- Inclusive wealth accounting
- Indirect taxes
- Investment
- ISIC (International Standard Industrial Classification)
- Intermediate production
- Market prices
- Operating surplus
- Primary factors of production
- Production approach
- Revision
- Shadow economy
- Stock
- Subsidy
- Value added

PART I

SHORT-TERM FLUCTUATIONS AND DEMAND MANAGEMENT

3. Earth's Business Cycle

Booms and busts are the tide of the Earth Economy. These fluctuations take place along the longer-term developments that we will discuss in Part II. The macroeconomic fluctuations typically turn up in changes of the reported rates of change of the economic variables. The rate of growth may, for example, slow down (and even turn negative), but then after some time usually a recovery sets in. These fluctuations constitute the business cycle that is the topic of this chapter. In order to get a better understanding we will first take a look at three key indicators of the business cycle for which we have data over a longer period: economic growth, inflation and unemployment.

In this chapter we will study the eartheconomic developments over the period 1980 – 2011. The choice for that period is pragmatic: the IMF World Economic Outlook (WEO) database readily provides the data for this period (and 2012 at the time of writing is still an estimate). With regard to another important indicator, the rate of unemployment, we will by necessity have to limit ourselves to a somewhat shorter period as estimates of the global rate of unemployment have only been provided by the International Labour Organization for a period starting in 1991, but as you will see we can also for this shorter period illustrate how short-term fluctuations in GPP relate to the planet's unemployment rate.

This Part focuses on these fluctuations and thus on the short run. We will use a longer time frame in Part II where we will analyse and discuss long-term growth and long wave theories.

3.1 FLUCTUATIONS IN GROSS PLANET PRODUCT

Let us first take a look at the fluctuations in Earth's production. Figure 3.1 shows the development of Gross Planet Product (GPP) since 1980. Figure 3.1a shows the level of Earth GPP (for which we will use the symbol Y) and Figure 3.1b shows the rate of change or growth rate of GPP ($\ddot{Y}$,). We will indicate rates of growth with a diaeresis (¨) so that $\ddot{A}$ indicates the rate of growth of the variable A over the period. The growth rate $\ddot{Y}$ is calculated as $GPP_t/GPP_{(t-1)} - 1$. The index t for time refers to the period of observation, so

$t - 1$ is the previous period. While we will almost always be using annual rates throughout this book (as we only have annual data) it is common to find reports for quarterly growth rates if the data are also available on a quarterly basis. This rate of change is generally reported as a percentage. For example, in 2007 and 2008 the levels of GPP were estimated at 55.7 and 61.2 trillion (that is: 10^{12}) US dollars, respectively. The rate of growth $\ddot{Y} = 61.2/55.7 - 1 = 0.099$ or 9.9%.

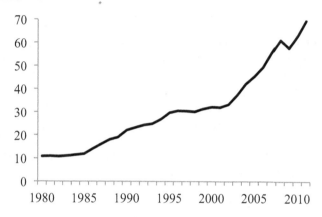

Source: IMF WEO April 2012 database

Figure 3.1a GPP 1980 – 2011 in trillions US\$, current prices

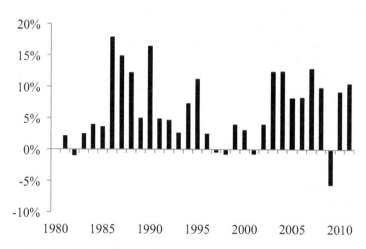

Source: IMF WEO April 2012 database

Figure 3.1b Growth rate of GPP 1980 – 2011

Figures 3.1a and 3.1b each provide a somewhat different perspective on the development of GPP. Figure 3.1a focuses attention more on the long run, showing the tremendous increase of GPP over the period 1980 – 2011. Three important phases of stagnation are evident in Figure 3.1a: the second oil crisis in the early 1980s, the period 1998 – 2002 when the Asian crisis and the dotcom crisis occurred and the financial crisis that started in 2007 and led to a substantial contraction of GPP in 2009. The recovery in 2010 and 2011 is sharp (the data for 2011 are still preliminary). In 2012 much attention focused on the possibility of a double dip. Note that it is much easier to see the short-term fluctuations when we focus on the annual rates of growth in Figure 3.1b, but also remember that basically the two figures are telling the same story.

Note that a positive growth rate in itself does not imply that the *status quo ante* (the situation before the disturbance) has been restored, as that would require a higher growth rate or a number of positive annual growth rates until the previous peak level has been reached again. Incidentally, this is a truism that many people tend to forget. You always need a stronger percentage increase to reach the previous peak. For example: your boss tells you that he will cut your salary by –50%, but that you need not worry because he will raise your salary by +50% afterwards. Note that the arithmetical average is zero, but that geometric average is –25%.

Exercise 3.1 Growth rates

- Calculate the year-on-year growth rates of Earth GPP for 2007/8 and 2008/9 using the following data in trillions of current US dollars.

Year	2007	2008	2009
GPP	55.7	61.2	57.8

- Next calculate the arithmetic and geometric annual averages of these growth rates over the full period 2007/9.
- Which of these two averages provides the best indication of average growth over 2007/2009?

Next consider Diagram 3.1. This diagram illustrates the standard methodology and the key measurement issues for the analysis of business cycles. The cycle shows a repeated pattern of ups and down around a trend (the dotted line). At some point in time the curve reaches its maximum (the peak) at which point the positive growth rate becomes negative. This is the start of the downturn. At the end of the collapse (the trough) the decline ends and the upswing starts and we have a positive growth rate again (although the economy obviously starts from a lower level than its peak value).

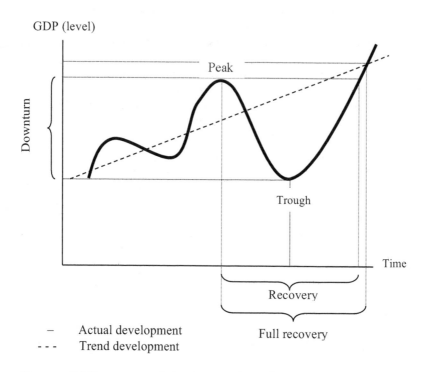

Diagram 3.1 Key concepts in business cycle analysis

The period that runs from the moment that we have negative growth until the economy reaches the previous peak level, is labelled 'Recovery'. (It could, however, be argued that full recovery may take even longer, namely until the trend level has been reached again – so exceeding the previous peak.)

Exercise 3.2 Recovery
  • Consider Figure 3.1a above and argue when full recovery from the recent financial crisis occurred.

Figures 3.2a (levels) and 3.2.b (annual growth rates) illustrate these basic concepts of business cycle analysis zooming in on Figures 3.1a and 3.1b and focusing on the years 1996 – 2002.

Exercise 3.3 Business cycle
- Use Figure 3.2a and 3.2b to locate peaks and troughs in GPP

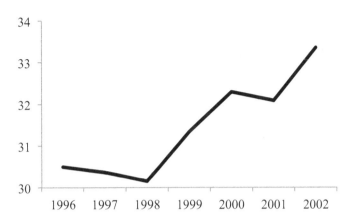

Source: IMF WEO April 2012 database

Figure 3.2a GPP 1996 – 2002, in trillions US$, current prices

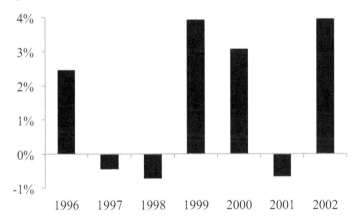

Source: IMF WEO April 2012 database

Figure 3.2b Annual growth rate of GPP (1996 – 2002)

3.2   EARTH INFLATION

It is important to realize that Figures 3.1 and 3.2 report nominal GPP (that is GPP in current prices) and that these variables will be influenced by increases of prices (inflation) and decreases of prices (deflation). Figure 3.3 shows the inflation rates for the period 1980 – 2011. We will discuss the pattern of inflation in the next section. Figure 3.4 reports the concomitant price levels using index numbers for the same years with the year 2000 as a base year (an index number is set at 100 in the base year).

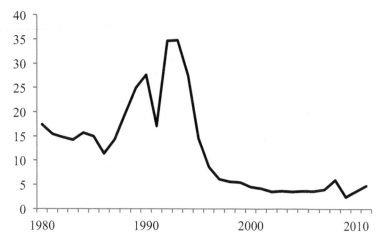

Source: IMF WEO April 2012 database (average consumer prices)

Figure 3.3 Earth inflation rates in per cent (1980 – 2011)

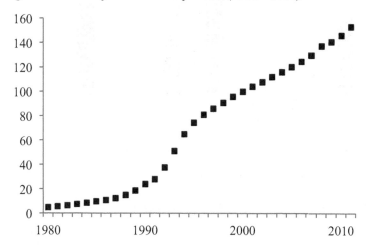

Source: Calculations based on IMF WEO April 2012 database

Figure 3.4 Earth Price Index Numbers (2000=100) 1980 – 2011

A price index number defines the general price level of goods and services in terms of prices in a specific year. The price index number thus reflects the price level and inflation reflects the rate of change in that price level. Several price index numbers exist, such as the Consumer Price Index and the GDP deflator. The GDP deflator relates to total GDP; consumption is one of the components of GDP and for other components statistical offices often calculate deflator series as well. (Note that we are not dealing with GDP, but with GPP and therefore we do not consider export and import prices). Index numbers in general are very useful summary indicators. This is especially true if we do not have unambiguous indications of the level of an economic variable but at the same time can be more confident about the relative changes that occur.

Text Box 3.1 Index numbers

Essentially an index number provides a relative (or percentage) indication of changes between levels that are observed between periods for some relevant period of time. Index numbers are calculated for prices, quantities, values and for any phenomenon that may be of interest. Index numbers are summary statistics that show deviations or changes of a quantity/number from a base observation..

   If, for example, the global emission of CO_2 in 1900 is 500 metric tons of carbon/year and 6500 metric tons of carbon/year in the year 2000, then the index number with 1900 as a base "(1900=100)" is 100 for the year 1900 and 1300 for the year 2000. Likewise the index number with base year 2000 is 100 for the year 2000 "(2000=100)" and 500/6500 = 7.7 for the year 1900. So we have:

Index number (year x =100) = observation / observation in year x

Most of the time we will study the development of real GPP or GPP in constant prices and its real growth rate that corrects for the changes in the purchasing power of money.

Let the price level at time t be P_t, so that a price index number in terms of base year "0" can be written as $P_t/P_{(t=0)}$ *100. We denote planet inflation (pi) by $\pi = P_t/P_{(t-1)} -1$ (multiply by 100 to get the inflation percentage). We can now deflate nominal GPP calculating real GPP in prices of the base year as $y = Y/P_{(t=0)}$ (note that real quantities will be written with small letters from now on and nominal values in capital letters). We can calculate real GPP growth $\ddot{y}$ using the exact expression $(1+\ddot{Y})/(1+\pi) - 1$. This expression can for relatively low rates of inflation and growth be approximated by $\ddot{y} = \ddot{Y} - \pi$.

Exercise 3.4 Inflation and real variables
- Why do the index numbers in Figure 3.4 continue to increase while Earth inflation according to Figure 3.3 comes down substantially?

Year	2006	2007	2008	2009
GPP deflator (2008 = 100)	84.9	92.1	100.0	96.6

- Calculate year-on-year inflation based on this deflator
- Use the data of exercise 3.1 and calculate GPP in constant 2008 prices
- Calculate real GPP growth in 2008 and 2009 from GPP in constant prices
- Calculate real GPP growth in 2008 and 2009 from nominal GPP growth and inflation using the exact formula $\ddot{y} = (1+\ddot{Y})/(1+\pi) - 1$ as well as the approximation $\ddot{y} = \ddot{Y} - \pi$

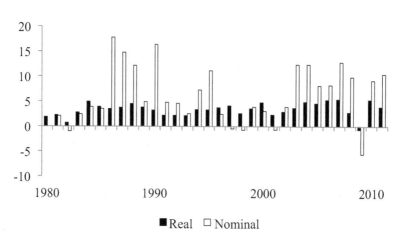

■ Real   □ Nominal

Source: Calculations based on IMF WEO April 2012 database
Note: 1980 nominal growth rate not available

Figure 3.5 Real and nominal annual GPP growth (1980 – 2011)

Figure 3.5 shows the impact of (not) deflating GPP growth rates in the period 1980 – 2011. Often the development of nominal GPP exacerbates the real changes, because prices rise when economic activity increases and prices decrease when the economy slows down. This is not the only reason why series have to be expressed in constant prices. Typically inflation is positive and therefore nominal expenditures almost always increase because the prices of products and services increase. The key issue of the analysis is whether the amount of goods and services available to the population increases or decreases and therefore the correction for inflation is necessary.

3.3   THREE DECADES OF GROWTH AND INFLATION

Figure 3.6 tells the combined story of inflation and real GPP growth. In this section we concentrate on the broad picture of the fluctuations and their potential drivers (note that we will discuss monetary policy issues in more detail in Chapter 7).

To start with, we see that Earth at the beginning of our period of observation in 1980 experienced a relatively high inflation rate as a consequence of the oil crises of the 1970s. Note, however, that inflation is already on a downward trend. The phenomenon of deceleration of inflation is called disinflation. This is to be distinguished from deflation when prices are decreasing. During a period of disinflation price levels still increase, but this increase is not as fast as before. The disinflation in the early 1980s is partially a consequence of the growth slowdown that we observe for real GPP.

From the mid 1980s to the mid 1990s inflationary experiences differ widely between regions. The common experience is that growth picks up and that commodity price shocks occur. The resurgence of Earth inflation in this period reflects the impact of change occurring in the emerging markets, in particular loose fiscal and monetary policies and bad policy responses to commodity price shocks. The early 1990s witness a global inflation explosion that is driven by the transition phase of the formerly centrally planned economies that move from administered prices to market prices that reflect scarcities.

Then around 1995 the period of the so-called Great Moderation sets in. Some observers attribute this to the almost universal adoption of better monetary policies, including central bank independence. Structural reforms and globalization are at least as important as they are bringing in competitive pressure and low cost producers. Earth inflation decreases to a stable level of about 5 per cent per annum while preserving economic growth. Some predict the end of macroeconomics. Around 2007 the Great Moderation, however, appears to end. The first indication is the upsurge of commodity prices that signals a new phase of globalization that entails fiercer competition for scarce resources.

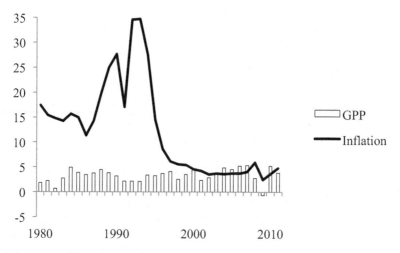

Source: IMF WEO April 2012 database

Figure 3.6 Real GPP growth and planet inflation (per cent, 1980 – 2011)

In 2009 real GPP growth turns negative as Earth experiences the Great Recession. The formal definition of a recession is a period at least two consecutive quarters of negative real GPP growth rates. This does not show up in the figures as they are based on annual data, but it is clear that 2009 is an exceptional year in the more than three decades that constitute our period of observation (see Banerji et al. 2012 on dating of the world business cycle). The Great Recession appears to be relatively short as growth already is restored in 2010, but it is still too early to tell if this brings a new structural break in the economic development of our planet: both 2011 and 2012 saw many discussions of a 'double dip' recession.

3.4   PLANET UNEMPLOYMENT

The development of unemployment rightly gets a lot of attention from policy makers and policy analysts. These discussions, however, are predominantly of a local (national) nature, although also here a global figure is reported (admittedly, it is not quoted by all international economic institutions). Since 1991 the International Labour Organization has reported the global unemployment rate, but often cautions that estimates are still preliminary. That caution implies that the reported level may as yet be less accurate than the *changes* in the level.

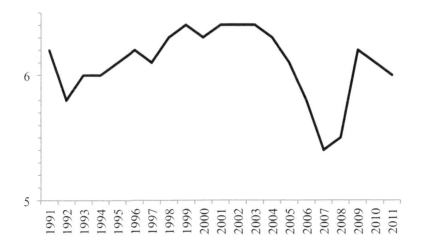

Source: ILO (2012a)

Figure 3.7 Earth unemployment rate in per cent (1991 – 2011)

There are many other reasons to consider the ILO unemployment rate as the pulse rate of the economy at best and not as an accurate measure of the extent of global unemployment. Unemployment is often hidden, for example, because people have a small job but would like to work longer or if they are self employed in the informal sector but would like to have a formal job. Even if they have a formal sector job, labour conditions may be very much substandard involving long working days, health hazards and other negative conditions that are not universally acceptable. For these reasons official statistics may provide poor indications of the need for proper employment. Still, with that caveat in mind, Figure 3.7 illustrates the decrease of unemployment that was setting in just before the Great Recession started: growth generated jobs at the global level and this reduced unemployment. The negative GPP developments in 2009 reduce demand for labour and the gains of 2005 – 2007 appear to have been lost overnight. The recovery in growth (Figure 3.5) is not sufficiently strong to enable Earth unemployment to return to pre-crisis levels. (Note that we will return to some of these issues in Chapter 8.)

Earth Economics

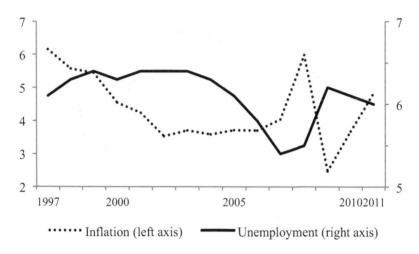

Sources: See Figures 3.5 and 3.7

Figure 3.8 Earth unemployment and inflation (1997 – 2011)

Figure 3.8 provides another perspective on unemployment linking it to planet inflation. From this perspective the reduction of unemployment signals scarcity and is associated with price increases in 2008. The Great Recession sharply brings down inflation, both on account of commodity price disinflation and wage moderation. Interestingly, inflation returns to pre-crisis levels rather quickly as GPP growth recovers, but employment recovers relatively slowly.

Business cycle research needs the most recent observations available. This is especially true in times of change. It is therefore useful to update the data that have been used in this textbook. Exercise 3.5 provides a recipe to help you prepare your own most up to date data set for the Earth economy.

Exercise 3.5 Prepare an up to date data set for the Earth economy
- Go to the data and statistics section of the IMF website at http://www.imf.org/external/data.htm.
- Select 'data'

You are now on a very useful page. Just take a look at what the IMF has to offer you. Sometimes access to these data sources is costly and you have to consult it via the library.

- Select 'World Economic Outlook Databases'.
- Select the most recent database.
- In the download section select 'By Country Groups (aggregated data)' and continue with the preparation or your report in four steps.
- Select 'World'.
- Select all series in the National Accounts data and the monetary sections.
- Set the data range at 1980 to the most recent year for which the data are not forecasted.
- Prepare and download the report.

Open the excel file and give it a preliminary check. The first thing to do is to check if the data are complete and read the descriptors carefully. Next the following steps are always useful.

- Calculate minimum and maximum values (and locate these in the series), averages, and standard deviations.
- Do the data make sense? Why are there four series for GDP? What is the difference? Remember that this is the kind of check that you always have to do when you use a data set.
- Graphical analysis of the data is an important step in the preliminary check of the data set. Getting a good feeling of the story in the data is also important because it will help you to think about the issues.
- Draw line diagrams of all series. Inspect the graphs. Ask yourself: is this what I expected to see? Are there anomalies? What is the story that the graph tells?

The data set contains different measures for key economic concepts (inflation, levels and growth rates of production). Take a look at two of the series for the level of GPP (note that this is still labelled GDP in the IMF data set

- Draw a line diagram for these two series.
- Draw preliminary conclusions! Where do the series agree; where do they differ?

3.5   KEY CONCEPTS

- Base year
- Constant prices
- Consumer Price Index (CPI)
- Current prices
- Deflation
- Deflator
- Disinflation
- Downturn
- Full recovery
- Great Moderation
- Great Recession
- Index number
- Inflation
- Nominal
- Peak
- Real growth
- Recession
- Recovery
- Stagnation
- *Status quo ante*
- Trend
- Trough
- Unemployment rate
- Upturn

4. Why $I = S$ and What That Means: The Building Blocks of Macroeconomic Analysis

Most macroeconomic analyses use conventions that make the calculations much easier and the analysis more transparent. One particularly useful abstraction is that we will deal with a one-good-economy in our analysis of the Earth economy. The economy both produces and consumes this good. People can eat it, can sleep and live in it, use it to go to work and there they can use the good to produce other goods. The distinguishing character of this 'one-goodness' is that the good is a consumption good if it is actually consumed and that it is an investment good if not (you will recognize that this convention fits in nicely with definitions applied in the Planet Accounts that we discussed in Chapter 2). Therefore, for example, an apple that is not consumed is an investment good since it is stored and inventories are by definition part of investment.

So by definition we have that production Q equals the total of consumption C and investment I so that $Q = C + I$. Since this equation follows from a definition (and thus always is true), we call this a definitional equation. In the same spirit, we define that a consumer can either spend his income on consumption or save so that saving equals the amount of income that is not consumed. This yields the definitional equation $Y = C + S$. Again by definition (you will recognize the Planet Accounts conventions again) $Q = Y$ and by implication we have $I = S$. (At this stage we do not include the government in our analysis yet; so there is no government spending and there are no taxes. Some think of this as Paradise before the Fall of Man).

Now it is important to realize that $I = S$ derived in this way is not an equilibrium condition at all. The equality is always true because it reflects the conventions and definitions of National Accounting. So *ex post* (that is: realized) values of investment always equal savings (remember that 'not consumed' equals both 'saved' and 'invested' by our definitions). It should thus not come as a surprise that the Earth data show this equality, if not exact then at least approximately. Figure 4.1 illustrates the development of Earth investment and Earth savings expressed in per cent of GPP. One reason to express these aggregates as shares in GPP is that ratios are more comparable over longer periods, because the nominator and denominator are influenced to the same extent by inflation. Note that the equality occurs both in upturns and downturns and in periods of high and low inflation.

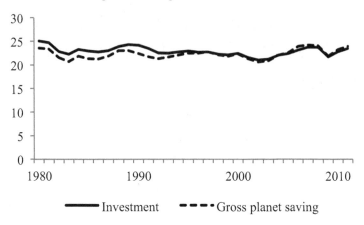

Source: IMF World Economic Outlook Database, April 2012

Figure 4.1   The condition I = S in the Earth economy (Gross planet saving and investment in per cent of GPP, 1980 – 2011)

Definitional equations such as $I = S$ can, however, sometimes be interpreted as equilibrium conditions because it is possible that *ex ante* (that is: planned or desired) investment is not equal to planned saving. Consider for example the *ex ante* disequilibrium situation where planned saving exceeds planned investment $(S > I)$. Since we know that saving is nothing more than income that is not consumed, consumption must be below its equilibrium level and thus inventories must be above their equilibrium level, that is: the inventories must exceed their planned levels as firms sell less than they expected. Firms obviously will want to reduce their production if their inventories exceed desired levels and thus income decreases until actual consumption equals planned consumption (and now we have $I = S$ again, both in the *ex ante* and in the *ex post* sense). The essential difference between this dynamic story and the boring Planet Accounts is that we now have introduced economic subjects. Their plans and acts are described in behavioural equations. Of course, we cannot observe the plans of firms and consumers directly, but we can see how the equilibrium changes and we can formulate hypotheses that express how we think economic behaviour is influenced by changes in economic variables.

4.1 CONSUMPTION

Let us, by way of example, think about consumption behaviour. A very basic assumption about consumption C is that it is positively related to income Y. If income increases then consumers will spend more so that consumption increases. If income decreases, consumers have less to spend and consumption goes down. After all, you need to have money in order to spend. However, people do not spend all their income. If their basic needs have been met, they will save part of their income. In the same vein, if they have no income, they still need to consume. This plausible story can be translated into a formal economic description. Let us assume that people always need to consume some amount C_0. This part of consumption is autonomous or exogenous (that is to say, it is independent of other variables; it is 'given' and we cannot or do not attempt to explain its level in our theory). Next we incorporate into our theory the idea that C is also a function of Y so that we have $C = cY + C_0$. The coefficient c is called the marginal propensity to consume or the marginal rate of consumption. Since consumption and income are positively related we know that $0 < c$ and because we assume that some part of income will be saved we know $c < 1$. Note that c is not the average rate of consumption C/Y but the marginal rate of consumption $\Delta C/\Delta Y$ where Δ indicates the change between two points of observation so $\Delta x = x_t - x_{t-1}$. We can express the same ideas mapping consumption as in Diagram 4.1.

Exercise 4.1 Marginal rate of consumption
- Explain why $c < 1$.
- Under what condition are marginal and average rate equal?

Consumption C

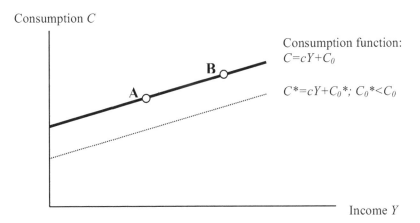

Consumption function:
$C = cY + C_0$

$C^* = cY + C_0^*; \; C_0^* < C_0$

Income Y

Diagram 4.1 A simple consumption function

When income increases consumption increases as is shown by the movement on the consumption function from point *A* to point *B*. This movement on the consumption curve reflects an endogenous process and is to be distinguished from changes in exogenous parameters that shift and/or rotate the curve. For example, a decrease in C_0 shifts the curve downwards to C^*.

Exercise 4.2 Consumption in the world economy
In this exercise you are asked to approximate a simple Keynesian consumption function $C = cY + C_0$ for the world economy. For the purpose of this exercise we assume the absence of a government sector. Use the database created in exercise 3.5
   •   Use GPP and savings rates to calculate savings and consumption.
   •   Calculate the average and marginal consumption rates for all years.
You can set Earth's marginal rate of consumption at 0.75.
   •   Determine a simple Keynesian consumption function for the most recent year.

4.2   OTHER CONSUMPTION THEORIES

In real life consumers do not decide about their expenditures on the basis of their current income alone. Over their lifetime people typically start with a level of consumption that exceeds their income (they borrow or the parents pick up the bill). Next follows a period in which income exceeds consumption: people repay their debt and start saving for their old age. Then they dissave. Diagram 4.2 illustrates this life cycle consumption pattern.

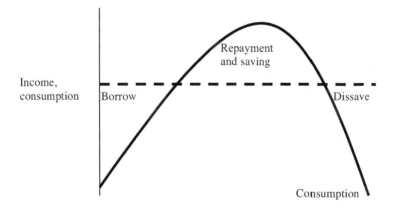

Diagram 4.2 Life cycle consumption pattern

Typically consumers will try to smooth the fluctuations in consumption and use their lifetime income to plan expenditures. This implies that consumers use their expected future income or permanent income as a beacon for current spending. By implication small and transient changes in current income will not exert a substantial influence on current consumption, because permanent income consists of a much longer stream of future earnings and is much less affected by transient changes. Changes in permanent income due to wage rate changes, employment situation, taxation and income transfers, however, influence all expected annual future incomes and thus current consumption to a large extent.

Exercise 4.3 Permanent income
- How does a cut in pension payments impact on current consumption?

The time perspective on consumption also implies that interest rates will have an impact. Essentially the interest rate is a reward for current consumption foregone. If the interest rate is high, the reward of forgoing consumption is high and this stimulates current saving. Interest is also an income component, but here the net asset position of the consumer matters. If the consumer is a debtor, her income (and thus her consumption) decreases if the interest rate increases; if the consumer has a net wealth position, his income will increase and thus his consumption rises. Another important new element that the time perspective brings in is the role of expectations. If consumers are pessimistic about the economic future they will reduce consumption (because their expected future income decreases) and this actually may work as a self-fulfilling prophecy.

4.3 SAVING – INVESTMENT AND GLOBAL SAVINGS GLUT

Consider a simple Keynesian consumption function $C = cY + C_0$ again, so that the saving function S equals $S = Y - C = (1 - c) Y - C_0$. This curve is illustrated in Diagram 4.3. For the moment we consider only autonomous investment I_0, so the investment function appears as the horizontal line $I = I_0$. Indeed, the behaviour of investment is not very exciting: our behavioural equation says that firms plan to invest a fixed amount independent of the state of the economy. The consumers in the economy, however, take the state of the economy into account and want to spend a part c of every extra unit of income Y. The economy is in equilibrium in point E, where the investment and saving functions intersect so that $I = S$. This can be illustrated as follows: in point *A* planned (or *ex ante*) saving would be in excess of investment and, as discussed earlier, inventories would build up. Firms thus would reduce their production in response to larger inventories so that GPP would be reduced and move in the direction of Y_E. This is a stable equilibrium because a disturbance of the equilibrium calls forth a tendency that restores equilibrium (that is: a movement towards the equilibrium).

Exercise 4.4 *I* = *S* (Diagram 4.3)
- Argue that a point to the left of point *E* is not an equilibrium point.
- In what direction does the economy adjust and why?
- Explain why saving can be negative.

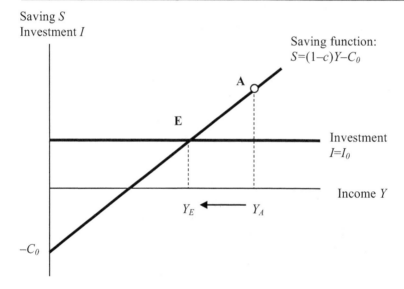

Diagram 4.3 I = S equilibrium in the Earth economy

Stability

Let us consider in somewhat more detail the issue of stability and instability of an equilibrium. If a temporary disturbance sets in motion movements away from the original point, the equilibrium is called unstable. If a system is characterized by a stable equilibrium then a temporary shock to the system will result in a temporary deviation from the equilibrium only, and eventually we will see that this system returns to the original starting point. The left hand panel of Diagram 4.4 illustrates such a stable equilibrium: the ball will always end up at the bottom of the valley. A temporary shock may, however, also result in a new equilibrium. The right hand panel of Diagram 4.4 shows an unstable equilibrium. It *is* an equilibrium: the ball is stable and lying on the top of the hill. Once a small disturbance, however, occurs it will roll down and never return to the original point. A special case occurs if a temporary shock does not end in a new stable equilibrium (this is different from the ball on the top of the hill that eventually will stop rolling when it reaches the bottom of the valley or a plain). Now the equilibrium and the system are unstable and a temporary shock will lead to an explosion or implosion of the system. It is thus important to establish the stability properties of an economy. If a solution is not stable, then it will only by luck and for a short term describe the economy. From a policy perspective, exploding or imploding economic variables can provide enormous difficulties. Examples of such instabilities are hyperinflation and unsustainable debt levels (that force people and nations to borrow ever increasing amounts).

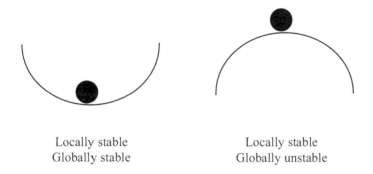

                Locally stable   Locally stable
                Globally stable   Globally unstable

Diagram 4.4 Different concepts of stability

The (in)stability of an equilibrium can be globally and locally defined as illustrated in Diagram 4.4. Note that 'equilibrium' is not by definition something good. For example, it is bad news when an economy gets stuck in a low-employment equilibrium.

Global Savings Glut

With the help of this simple model we are already able to shed some light on the policy debate on the cause of the financial and economic crisis. One of the key topics in the debate is the idea of a global savings glut: Earth's population saved too much and that caused the problems. It is not directly intuitively clear that saving can be bad for the economy. This is because many earthlings suffer from the Fallacy of Composition. This fallacy is the logical error of inferring that something must be true at the aggregate level of the macro economy from the fact that it is true at the individual level (micro economy). A well-known example of the fallacy is the Paradox of Thrift. Increasing saving is good for an individual, but it may hurt global welfare if everybody wants to increase saving. Consider Diagram 4.3. An increase in saving can be brought about in two ways: a decrease in autonomous consumption C_0 which shifts the saving function upwards and a decrease in the consumption rate c (which equals $1 - s$, where s is the savings rate) rotating the savings function upward to the left with $(0, -C_0)$ serving as a hinge. In both cases, saving reduces income. This is a sobering paradox, but a brighter picture for saving exists as well and – interestingly – in the same model. Increase I_0 so that Y increases. Therefore, an economy can save and become better off provided that it decides to invest more (and then saving will increase endogenously). Our simple model therefore already provides us with an answer on the question of how to escape from the modern Paradox of Thrift that motivates the theorists of the global saving glut. The key is to increase investment!

4.4   THE MULTIPLIER

It is interesting to see how an exogenous shock works out in this system. We start with a simple Keynesian consumption function $C_t = cY_t + C_0$ and set the marginal consumption rate or propensity to consume at 0.8 and autonomous consumption C_0 at 750 billion (these values are roughly in line with the data for the Earth economy according to Exercise 4.2). So the simple Keynesian consumption function can be written as $C_t = 0.8\,Y_t + 750$. Now let us assume that Earth investment increases exogenously by 100 billion. The direct impact is that GPP increases by 100. The increase in income generates extra consumption of $0.8*100 = 80$ and GPP increases by the same amount generating another (second order) increase of consumption by $0.8*80 = 64$ and so on. In the end the increase in autonomous investment yields an increase in GDP of 100 $(1+0.8+0.8^2+0.8^3+0.8^4+\ldots\ 0.8^n) = 100*5 = 500$ billion. The impulse to the Earth economy (including the original increase of 100) is due to the multiplier effect which in this simple model equals $1 + c + c^2 + c^3 + c^4 + \ldots\ c^n$ or $1/(1-c) = 1/(1-0.8) = 1/0.2 = 5$.

We can of course also arrive at this result by solving the model. The model consists of four equations (note that we always need to have exactly as many endogenous variables as we have equations and *vice versa*). The complete model is written as:

Consumption function:	$C = cY_t + C_0$	(4.1)
Definition equation:	$S = Y - C$	(4.2)
Investment function:	$I = I_0$	(4.3)
Equilibrium condition:	$I = S$	(4.4)

Endogenous: Y, C, I, S
Exogenous: c, I_0, C_0

Combining equations (4.1) – (4.4), we solve $S = Y - C = (1 - c)Y_t - C_0 = I_0$ or $(1 - c)Y_t = I_0 + C_0$. Now we can write the reduced form equation (that describes how an endogenous variable depends on the model's exogenous parameters only) for Y as $(I_0 + C_0)/(1 - c)$ in which we recognize the Keynesian multiplier $1/(1 - c)$ again. Note that reduced form equations can be derived for all endogenous variables. The reduced form equation, for example, for C equals $c(I_0 + C_0)/(1 - c) + C_0$ which again expresses the endogenous variable C in terms of the model's exogenous parameters. The reduced form equation for I is in this case a very simple $I = I_0$.

Exercise 4.5 Stability
Assume that investment is a positive function of GPP so that we have the following expression: $I_t = I_0 + \alpha Y_t$ and $\alpha > 0$ and use $S = (1 - c)Y_t - C_0$ with as before $0 < c < 1$.
- Derive the equilibrium condition graphically and mathematically
- Analyse the stability of the equilibrium

One of the implications of the multiplier is that fluctuations in the exogenous components C_0 and I_0 are magnified so that larger fluctuations of production and income result. Especially in the context of a financial and economic crisis consumers may reduce their expenditures. This is true both endogenously because national income decreases and exogenously because consumers decide to save more (read: consume less) independently of the level of their income (this is a reduction of C_0) and because they may want to save more out of their income (a decrease in c). Firms will change their investment plans (so a reduction in I_0 in our model).

Exercise 4.6 Multiplier
- Derive from the data set of the Earth economy (Exercise 3.5) by how much Investment and GPP decreased in 2009 (*vis-à-vis* 2008).
- What does this suggest with respect to the investment multiplier?

4.5   A SHORT DIGRESSION ON NOTATIONS AND GRAPHICAL REPRESENTATIONS

In order to keep the analysis simple and straightforward this book uses explicit and linear behavioural equations. Economists can, however, also be very general in the functions that they use. For example the consumption function would then be $C = C(Y)$ with $C' > 0$ where C' is the first derivative of C with respect to Y or $\partial C/\partial Y$ or C_Y. Sometimes authors use $+$ and $-$ signs below the arguments of a function to indicate whether the first derivative is positive or negative.

In all the above cases we only impose that consumption increases as income increases, but when we use these general functions this need not be in a linear way (it is still a possibility). Two arbitrary examples of functions that could be described by the notation are $C=\beta\sqrt{Y} + \theta$ or $C =\lambda \ln Y + \gamma$. Clearly then, this notation is more general indeed. We can now write the model (equations 4.1 – 4.4) in this chapter as:

$$C=C(Y) \tag{4.1'}$$
$$S = Y - C \tag{4.2'}$$
$$I = I_0 \tag{4.3'}$$
$$I = S \tag{4.4'}$$

As before we need as many endogenous variables as we have equations and *vice versa*; in this case as before Y, C, I and S are endogenous, while I_0 is the only explicit and exogenous variable. It is helpful to rewrite the model in differentials as $dI = dY - dC = (1 - \partial C/\partial Y)dY$ so that we have again the familiar multiplier $dY/dI = 1/(1 - \partial C/\partial Y)$.

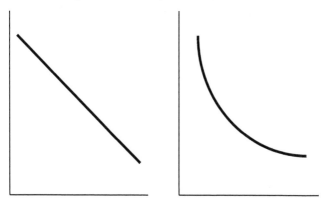

Diagram 4.5 Linear (left) and non-linear (right) curve

In the same vein almost all diagrams in Part I use linear functions (straight lines), but in line with the more general notation, we could also use curves of course (Diagram 4.5).

Yet another graphical representation is often encountered that depicts the economic processes using arrows and boxes where boxes are used to represent variables and arrows indicate the direction of the causal influence of one variable on another. Plusses and minuses are used to show whether this relationship is positive or negative. So a relationship that entails that *B* increases (decreases) when *A* decreases (increases) can be represented by

Diagram 4.6 provides a graphical representation of our simple model. Note that investment is exogenous since no arrow points at the investment box. Planetary income and consumption are endogenous variables and there is a feedback loop from consumption to national income that represents the multiplier process (only in equilibrium this feedback loop becomes zero).

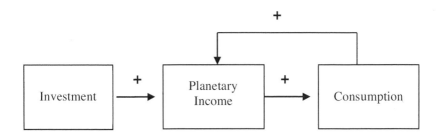

Diagram 4.6 Graphical representation of multiplier process

4.6 KEY CONCEPTS

- Average consumption rate
- Autonomous
- Behavioural equation
- Definitional equation
- Endogenous
- Equilibrium
- Ex ante
- Exogenous
- Ex post
- Fallacy of Composition
- Global stability

- Instability
- Life cycle model
- Local stability
- Marginal consumption rate
- Multiplier
- One-good-economy
- Paradox of Thrift
- Permanent income
- Propensity to consume
- Reduced form equation
- Second order effect

5. Investment, the IS Curve, and Product Market Equilibrium

Economists like to think about investment primarily in terms of enabling or enlarging future production, but that is not always the case. Investment by definition equals the amount of production that is not consumed and there is no reason why this should always be done with the aim of future production. Very visible, but unproductive investments include the pyramids, Stonehenge and the Eiffel Tower. Consumption has been deferred for religious reasons and to create symbols of (economic) power. This manner of investment is clearly exogenous and we will not attempt to explain it. So far, we have treated all investment as a completely exogenous variable. This is an unsatisfactory situation because investment is clearly influenced by economic variables and because, as discussed in the previous chapter, fluctuations in investment via the multiplier are an important determinant of the fluctuations in GPP that make up the Earth's business cycle. In this chapter investment will become endogenous (so we are going to explain the level of investment in a theory represented by a model). There are many theories about investment (a selection is discussed in Section 5.3), but initially we narrow the range of explanations and analyse only how investment decisions are being influenced by the interest rate R.

Typically an investment flow will require an upfront payment (a negative cash flow, that is: the investment I) at the beginning of the project followed by receipts (positive cash flows). We can write these cash flows as CF_t, where (t =1, 2, 3, ..., n) and n is the time span of the investment project. For example: an initial investment has to be made of 35 and then in the next four years a return of 10 is generated. This will generate net receipts of 5, so there is a profit. But is it worth the trouble? In order to be able to answer this question we should consider an alternative, namely the opportunity costs that consist of the returns in case something else had been done with the investment fund. If the investment would not have been made, the money could have been put on a saving deposit. Suppose the interest rate is 10%, so that 35 saving would generate $35 \times 1.10^4 = 51.24$. The investment project makes less money than the alternative and a rational profit-maximizing firm will therefore not invest. In general, a firm will invest if the Net Present Value (NPV) of the discounted cash flows is positive so if

$$-I + \frac{CF}{1+R} + \frac{CF_2}{(1+R)^2} + \frac{CF_3}{(1+R)^3} + \cdots + \frac{CF_n}{(1+R)^n} > 0$$

An increase in R makes the future cash flows less valuable (they are discounted more heavily) so that some potential investment projects will have a lower NPV. At higher R the amount of investment funds will thus *ceteris paribus* (all else equal) be lower (see for example Diagram 5.1; the NPV becomes negative around an interest rate of 6 per cent and the investment will not take place for higher rates).

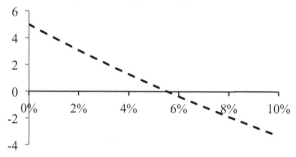

Diagram 5.1 NPV of an investment of 35 at t = 0 with four positive payoffs of 10 in the periods t = 1, 2, 3 and 4 for different interest rates

Thus, we find a negative or inverse relationship between investment I and interest R.

Exercise 5.1 Investment function
- Check in Diagram 5.1 the intersection with the vertical axis.

5.1   WORLD INVESTMENT

We can also observe a negative relationship between investment and R at the aggregate planetary level. Figure 5.1 by way of illustration plots Earth's investment to GPP ratio (I/Y) against a representative real long-term interest rate (so after correction for inflation). You should note that Figure 5.1 is not the investment function that we will use in this chapter, that the figure provides only a bivariate analysis and that other potentially relevant explanatory variables thus have not been considered. With this caveat in mind, Figure 5.1 illustrates that lower levels of interest are associated with stronger investment.

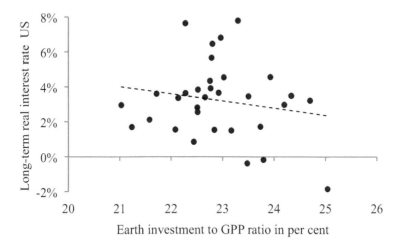

Sources: IMF World Economic Outlook April 2012 database and OECD 2012, Main Economic Indicators database (US government bond yield; 10 year)

Figure 5.1 Earth's investment (in 1980 prices) versus long-term US interest rate in per cent, 1980 – 2011

Text Box 5.1 Elasticity

An elasticity is a summary measure that provides an indication of the strength of the relationship between two variables. The elasticity is defined as the ratio of the relative change of the dependent variable to the relative change of the explanatory variable. In the case of the interest rate elasticity of investment we thus take the ratio of $\Delta I/I$ to $\Delta R/R$. So we have

$$\varepsilon_R^I = \frac{\frac{\Delta I}{I}}{\frac{\Delta R}{R}} \quad \text{or} \quad \frac{\Delta I}{\Delta R}\frac{R}{I}$$

If the absolute value of an elasticity is smaller than 1 we call the relationship inelastic and for absolute values larger than 1 it is elastic. Two extreme cases occur: if the elasticity is 0 the relationship is perfectly inelastic and it is perfectly elastic when $\varepsilon = \infty$

We write a new investment function as $I = I_0 - iR$ where i reflects the interest rate sensitivity and $i > 0$. This function states that a higher interest rate reduces the level of *ex ante* planned investment.

Exercise 5.2 Elasticity
- We have the following investment function $I = I_0 - iR$ with $I_0 = 40$ and $i = 4$.
- Draw a diagram of the investment function and calculate the interest rate elasticity of investment at R of 0, 4, 5 and 8.
- What is the interest rate elasticity of investment at $R = 10$?

We can now derive an expression that relates Y to the interest rate. First write down the model:

Consumption function:	$C_t = cY + C_0$	(5.1)
Definition equation:	$S = Y - C$	(5.2)
Investment function:	$I = I_0 - iR$	(5.3)
Equilibrium condition:	$I = S$	(5.4)

Endogenous: Y, C, I, S
Exogenous: c, I_0, C_0, R

Next we solve the model starting with $S = Y - C = (1 - c)Y - C_0 = I = I_0 - iR$ and find Y as $(I_0 + C_0)/(1 - c) - iR/(1 - c)$. Since we take R to be exogenous at this point of the analysis, this expression is the reduced form equation for Y.

Exercise 5.3 Reduced form equation
- Derive the reduced form equation for S
- How is S influenced in this model by an increase in R?

5.2   THE I = S SCHEDULE

We can plot the relationship between the income level and the interest rate in order to derive the $I = S$ (or simply IS) curve. This curve shows the combinations of Y and R for which we have macroeconomic equilibrium in the product market (Diagram 5.2). Starting again from $S = Y - C$ in order to set $S = (1 - c)Y - C_0 = I = I_0 - iR$ we can now solve for R and then obtain the expression $R = (I_0 + C_0)/i - (1 - c)/i \cdot Y$. We draw the IS curve in (Y, R) space (see Diagram 5.2). The IS curve slopes downward since $1 - c > 0$ and $i > 0$, but note that the IS curve can become vertical (if $i \rightarrow \infty$) or horizontal (if $i \downarrow 0$ or $c \uparrow 1$). If the interest rate decreases, we get a movement on the curve as from point A to point B in Diagram 5.2. The economic intuition is that an increase in R reduces investment I and by the multiplier process this reduces production. An alternative reasoning is that since we have equality of saving and investment, saving must be reduced if higher R induces lower investment and this by necessity requires lowering of Y. Thus, we have in our model a negative relationship between R and Y.

Interest R

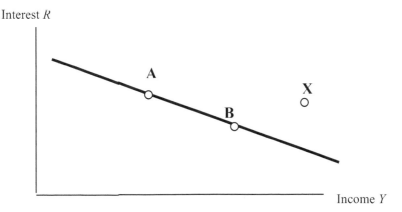

Income Y

Diagram 5.2 The IS curve

Exercise 5.4 Interest rate elasticity
- Discuss the interest rate elasticity of the IS curve in the case of a vertical IS curve.
- Answer the same question, but now for a horizontal IS curve.

In addition to this endogenous process, changes in the exogenous factors will of course also be relevant. The IS function shifts to the right due to autonomous increases in investment and consumption and it becomes steeper if c decreases. A change in i gives a combination of a shift and a rotation of the IS curve.

Exercise 5.5 Shifting the IS curve
- Analyse the impact of a reduction in C_0 on the locus of the IS curve.
- Also analyse the impact of an increase in i.

Now what does it mean if a point is not on the IS curve, as for example point X in Diagram 5.2? The IS curve represents the equilibrium combinations of Y and R. In point X, the interest rate is too high for an equilibrium given the level of Y that point X represents. *Ex ante* or planned investment I in point X will thus be smaller than S (saving is determined by

Y) and equality between *I* and *S* requires a reduction of *Y* and thus a movement of *X* to the left until the IS curve is reached. By the same reasoning, points to the left of the IS curve are characterized by *I* > *S* so that inventories are below planned levels and firms will increase production so that income rises. This reasoning establishes that the equilibria that are represented by the IS curve are stable.

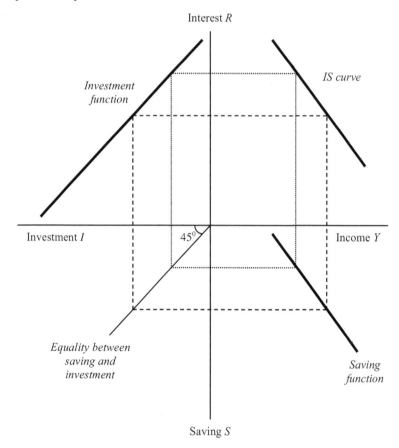

Diagram 5.3 Graphical derivation of the IS curve

Diagram 5.3 graphically illustrates the relationships that simultaneously build the IS curve. Note that some of the quadrants in the diagram appear to be upside down: measurement always starts in the origin and all variables are positive (so, for example, if we move down the *S* axis saving increases). In the North West quadrant, we have the investment function. Lower *R* yields higher *I* (note that this is moving to the left in the mirrored diagram). In the

South West quadrant we find the equality $I = S$ that is represented by a 45° line. In the South East quadrant we have the savings schedule that shows that higher Y yields higher S. As shown by the dotted lines the IS curve in the North East quadrant represents combinations of R and Y where we have equilibrium between saving and investment.

Exercise 5.6 Autonomous spending and IS curve
- Use Diagram 5.3 to analyse the impact of an autonomous increase in investment.
- Use Diagram 5.3 to analyse the impact of an autonomous increase in consumption.

5.3   OTHER INVESTMENT THEORIES

So far we have been concerned with a simple investment function that only takes exogenous investment plans and the interest rate into account. The reason for keeping things simple is that the interest rate is a price that results on the money market that we will study in Chapter 7. We will stick to the simple investment-interest relationship in the remainder of this book, but only for ease of exposition. It is important to recognize that many investment theories exist that look beyond this simplicity because in the real world many investment motives exist. This section discusses four of these theories.

The starting point of any investment decision is that it should have a positive pay off. Investors will invest in labour saving technologies if the wage rate is high and abstain from such investment if the costs of capital are high. Once the investment is done the technology is locked as it is incorporated in the capital goods that have been produced or purchased. Typically, wage moderation slows down the incorporation of labour reducing technology.

Adjustment Costs Theory

Adjusting capital goods is, however, a costly process. Especially if capital goods have to be disposed, costs may run high, but other costs are also relevant. For example, a firm that has to lay off personnel will incur administrative costs, while firing employees also means that part of the human capital of the firm is lost. Re-hiring will involve management time, on the job training and administrative costs again. The same is *a fortiori* true for scrapping and moth balling of machinery and other capital goods. Firms will therefore try to avoid the costs of fluctuations in the production level. One way to smooth production fluctuations *vis-à-vis* demand fluctuations is to maintain inventories as a buffer against demand shocks.

Inventory Theory

The adjustment costs theory thus provides a rationale for the existence of inventories. (Changes in inventories are part of investment and thus their behaviour is relevant if we want to study investment.) As changes in capacity are costly, it may pay to have inventories. Inventories are not only maintained to smooth fluctuations in demand, but also to ensure that intermediate products are available. Just in time deliverance of intermediate products makes a firm vulnerable to upstream accidents and fluctuations. A strike or a natural disaster may disturb the value chain so that downstream producers can no longer produce.

Inventories are, however, not a free lunch and entail costs such as the interest over the working capital incorporated in the inventory goods and the cost of storage, insurance and loss. Clearly the optimal level of inventories will have to reflect these costs as well as the firm's expectations about future demand (note that we will discuss inventories also from a truly long term perspective in Chapter 12 when we discuss the long economic waves).

Accelerator Theory

The accelerator theory of investment states that investment increases when GPP increases (Exercise 4.4 provides a rough and ready example). Firms, for example, will make their investment decision on the basis of the expected development of the economy. If the outlook is good, investment will rise. This investment creates extra production capacity and GPP will rise even further stimulating additional investment (this is the accelerator). The downside of the process is that investment decreases when GPP decreases, reducing production capacity and thereby putting an additional drag on GPP.

Animal Spirits Theory

The Animal Spirits theory derives directly from Keynes's *General Theory* and relates mainly to changes in perceptions and expectations of businessmen. As such this theory is mainly reflected in changes in the autonomous component of investment (that is: I_0 in our earlier discussions).

> (I)ndividual initiative will only be adequate when reasonable calculation is supplemented and supported by animal spirits, so that the thought of ultimate loss which often overtakes pioneers, as experience undoubtedly tells us and them, is put aside as a healthy man puts aside the expectation of death. This means,

unfortunately, not only that slumps and depressions are exaggerated in degree, but that economic prosperity is excessively dependent on a political and social atmosphere which is congenial to the average business man. (Keynes 1936, p. 162)

The investment herding behaviour of firms is also reflected in modern theories of uncertainty (if firms perceive higher risks in general they will reduce investment), contamination and over-optimism. Contamination is particularly relevant for investment in specific analytical country groups or regions; even countries that have no problems at all will often be treated as bad investment opportunities if problems occur in countries that belong to their group. Contamination can also take place at the level of industries. The volatility of the global autonomous investment component is amplified via the multiplier and reflected in substantial volatility of GPP. On the other hand, over-optimism can act as an important stimulus for growth and innovation (Kahneman 2011, Chapter 24). In Chapter 12 we will discuss Kondratieff's theory of the long wave that partially reflects on all these factors.

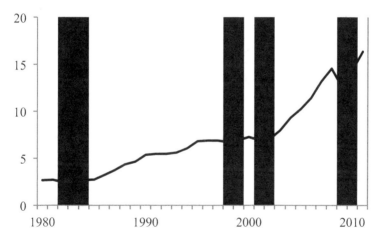

Source: Calculations based on IMF World Economic Outlook database, April 2012.

Figure 5.2 Decreases in gross planet investment (trillions of US$) lead recessionary periods (shaded areas)

Figure 5.2 illustrates how periods of decreasing investment result in decreases of GPP (the grey areas in the figure show recessionary periods in which GPP levels are below their previous peak level). The figure suggests that causality runs from global investment behaviour to GPP as the drop in investment precedes the recessionary periods.

5.4   KEY CONCEPTS

- Accelerator
- Adjustment costs of investment
- Animal spirits
- *Ceteris paribus*
- Downstream production
- Elastic

- Elasticity
- Inelastic
- Net Present Value
- Upstream production
- Perfectly elastic
- Perfectly inelastic

6. What About Government?

The existence of national governments is probably the most important reason why eartheconomics is not yet practised everywhere. Realists state that governments pursue national interests and therefore a model that focuses on the whole will miss that policy coordination amongst the parts is difficult. International coordination of national economic policies is especially difficult since many opinions around the globe exist about the appropriateness of economic policies. The realist view has a valid point of course, but for eartheconomics the aggregate behaviour is all that ultimately matters. Sometimes a fuzzy picture emerges when countries follow completely different and contradictory policies so that on average the impulse from government at the world level is about zero. However, many instances exist where we can observe that the aggregate of governments (and their problems and solutions) moves in the same direction. In the 'Golden Age' of the 1950s and 1960s, for example, policies by and large were Keynesian. The oil crises in 1973 and 1980s led to stagflation (a combination of high inflation and high unemployment that could not be cured by Keynesian policies). Ultimately this failure provided the basis for structural reform policies and the Washington Consensus which both put a lot of weight on markets. The initial response to the financial and economic crisis in 2009 is the most recent example of a case of national policies moving in the same direction. The debt problems that started to emerge in large parts of the world economy in 2010 – 2012 similarly result in a quite general movement of policies towards austerity measures (ILO, 2012b)

Consider Figure 6.1 that illustrates the global policy response to the Great Recession. National economies differed to some extent in the exact policy mix (that is the combination of fiscal and monetary policy instruments), but a very large majority of the countries opted for fiscal loosening (or fiscal stimulus or expansionary fiscal policies) by reducing taxes and/or increasing government spending (Figure 6.2, we will return to monetary policy in Chapter 7, but for now you may want to note that monetary policy has also been loose in the vast majority of countries in 2009).

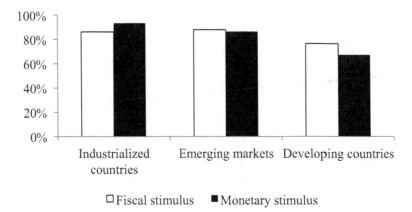

□ Fiscal stimulus   ■ Monetary stimulus

Sources: World Bank (2010), Fig. 3.17, p. 82 and *OECD Observer* No 280, 2010,
              pp. 22 – 37

*Figure 6.1   Policy mix in 2009 (percentage of countries with stimulating
              monetary and fiscal policies)*

The tsunami of fiscal expansion in 2009 marks a break in policies that
aimed at reducing the public deficit (government expenditures minus
revenues; see Figures 6.2 and 6.7). Indeed, for long stabilization or
Keynesian demand management policies were not *en vogue* around the globe,
but since the start of the Great Recession many previous positions are being
reconsidered. Therefore, it pays to take a closer analytical look at what all
these government activities mean from the short-term Earth perspective that
is developed in this Part of the book.   Before doing so, however, it is
important to note that the role of government extends well beyond its short-
term impact on effective demand. Government sets rules and regulations and
provides security that are all essential for economic activity. Government
invests in infrastructure, education and health, which are all essential for
development and growth in the long run. We will return to some of these
questions in later Parts: for now our focus is on the short-term impact of
government expenditures, receipts and debt.

6.1   BRINGING GOVERNMENT INTO THE EQUATIONS

The analysis of government changes the equilibrium condition from $I = S$
into $I + G = S + T$ where G is government spending and T is taxes. It is easy
to see why this is the case. We now have $C + I + G = Y = C + S + T$ as a

definition equation. The left hand side describes what goods are produced: consumer goods C (everything the consumer buys), government expenditure G and private investment I that as before consists of fixed capital formation and the change in inventories. The right hand side of the definition equation describes how income is spent: everybody first has to pay taxes T and the money that is not spent on consumption C is saved. Subtract C from both sides of the definition equation and the new equilibrium condition emerges.

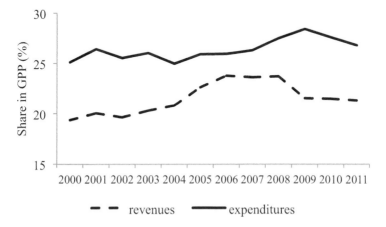

Source: ILO Work of World Dataset 2012

Figure 6.2 Government expenditure and revenue shares in GPP (per cent, 2000 – 2011)

We can write this equilibrium condition of course also as $S - I = G - T$ and then we see directly that investment can exceed private saving if taxes exceed government expenditure. Yet another formulation, namely $I = S + T - G$, directly clarifies that investment equals private saving plus public saving. Public saving equals receipt minus expenditure (the same is true of course for everybody). If public saving is positive, we have a budget surplus and if it is negative, we have a budget deficit. So if we introduce the government, we need to tackle three issues: government spending, taxes and government debt (because a budget deficit needs to be financed and repaid in later years).

Government Spending

Government spending does not create new analytical difficulties for the moment; because we will treat it as an exogenous variable most of the time and the analysis of a change of exogenous government spending shifts the IS curve in the same way as increases in autonomous consumption and autonomous investment. So if government spending is permanently reduced the IS curve shifts inward to the left. In our model we simply add the 'behavioural equation' $G=G_0$. So we can treat government spending for now as one of the exogenous components of effective demand.

Taxation

Taxation can be treated in several ways (we can assume that it is constant, proportional to income or we can think of progressive taxes when the average tax to GDP ratio increases for higher income), but we always need to make sure that somebody pays the taxes. So we set disposable income Y^D at $Y - T$ and adjust the consumption function accordingly so that we get the following expression: $C = cY^D + C_0 = c(Y - T) + C_0$.

We can distinguish three cases: lump sum taxes that do not depend on the level of income and/or wealth (so $T = T_0$), proportional taxes that increase with increases in income (so $T = tY$ with t the average and in this case also marginal tax rate with $0 < t < 1$) and progressive taxes that have a tax exemption – that is an income level below which one does not have to pay taxes (so $T = tY - T_0 > 0$; see Diagram 6.1 for a graphical representation).

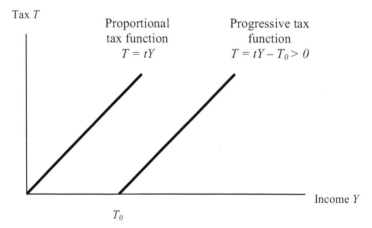

Diagram 6.1 Proportional and progressive tax schedules

Exercise 6.1 Taxation
- Explain why Diagram 6.1 shows proportional/progressive taxation.
- At what income level are progressive taxes payable?
- Draw a lump sum tax in Diagram 6.1.
- Draw a diagram of average and marginal tax rates for a lump sum tax, for proportional and for progressive taxation.

Text Box 6.1 The Islamic tax system of Zakat

Often people think that progressive taxation is an invention of modern times, possibly a social democratically inspired system aiming at redistribution. This is a misconception. One of the oldest, still surviving and very stable systems of taxation is *Zakat* (a religious Islamic tax installed by the Prophet in the 7th century). *Zakat* has many properties of progressive taxation. The tax rate is low at 2.5% and applied to most forms of monetary wealth and earned income, but with many clear and regulated exemptions, for example, regarding the *Nisad*. The Islamic *Nisad* is the 7th century equivalent of the modern world's tax exemption. The *Nisad* is expressed in many ways, for example, by the minimum number of camels and goats, the threshold value on produce of land distinguished by agricultural technology, or the grams of gold and silver that a faithful can earn or own before the tax is calculated over the remaining surplus.

Exercise 6.2 Taxation in the Model
- Write down the model with proportional taxation and exogenous government expenditure.
- Solve the model and determine the reduced form equation for *Y*.
- Calculate the multiplier for exogenous investment and compare this with the case of a closed economy without government.
- Why does it differ?

6.2 GOVERNMENT MULTIPLIERS

We use the model that was developed in Chapter 5 as a basis. For a starter we will assume that both taxes and government expenditures are exogenous ($G = G_0$ and $T = T_0$). Solve $I + G = S + T$ for Y; use $s = 1 - c$; and set

$$I_0 - iR + G_0 = s Y^D + T_0 = (1 - c)(Y - T_0) - C_0 + T_0 = (1 - c)Y - C_0 - cT_0$$

in order to get the reduced form equation:

$$Y = (I_0 + C_0 + G_0 - cT_0)/(1 - c) - iR/(1 - c).$$

We can see directly that an increase in exogenous government expenditure *ceteris paribus* increases GPP while an increase in lump sum taxation decreases GPP. Note that the multipliers for government expenditure and taxation do not only differ in sign but also in magnitude. For government expenditure, we have a multiplier of $1/(1 - c)$, but for taxation, the multiplier is also smaller in absolute value: $c/(1 - c)$ so that an extra unit of government expenditure does more good than a unit extra taxation hurts. Basically, this is because government spends and people both spend and save. This principle is reflected in policy discussions where budget neutrality is often an important issue (budget neutrality requires that government spends exactly what it receives so that $G = T$). This problem is easy to solve because $I + G = S + T$ reduces simply to $I = S$ (but note that this does not yield the economy without government of Chapter 5!).

Text Box 6.2 Check your maths the easy way

Note two easy ways to check your mathematics. The trick is always to find out parameters that you can set equal to zero or one (so as to take away as much complicating calculus as possible) and then check if the mathematical result intuitively still makes sense. Let's do this with the previous section. First, set $T_0 = 0$ and check that you get the original multipliers without government. (Of course you do not get the same reduced form equation for Y; because setting $T_0 = 0$ in this case implies that government runs a budget deficit).

Second trick: 'start from the other side'. This recipe means that rather than using $I + G = S + T$ you use $Y = C + I + G$ as a check. Now we have as our point of departure $Y = c(Y - T_0) + C_0 + I_0 - iR + G_0$ so that you again find that

$$Y(1 - c) = -cT_0 + C_0 + I_0 - iR + G_0$$

and

$$Y = (I_0 + C_0 + G_0 - cT_0)/(1 - c) - {}^{iR}/(1 - c).$$

With proportional taxation and a balanced budget we have to solve

$$I_0 - iR + G = I_0 - iR + tY = S + T = (1 - c)(Y - tY) - C_0 + tY \text{ or}$$

$$I_0 - iR = (1 - c)(1 - t)Y - C_0$$

and the reduced form is: $Y = (I_0 + C_0)/\{(1 - c)(1 - t)\} - iR/\{(1 - c)(1 - t)\}$.

Note that the denominator is smaller than before (for example for $c = 0.8$ and $t = 0.25$ the denominator is $0.2 \cdot 0.75 = 0.15$ so the balanced budget multiplier is $1/0.15 = 6^2/_3$. This is larger than the closed economy without government case that we calculated earlier. It is easy to see why the multiplier is larger: the reason is that government completely spends every extra unit of taxation whereas consumers would only spend a part (namely c). Therefore, taxing 1 unit of income away from a consumer directly increases government expenditure (and thus income) by +1 and directly reduces consumption (and thus income) by $-c$ so that income initially on balance increases by $(1 - c)$ and this sets the multiplier process in motion.

6.3   INCOME (RE)DISTRIBUTION

One of the issues that a world government has to address is an equitable or fair distribution of income. Government uses taxes, subsidies and income transfers to influence this distribution.

Poverty

Let us first take a look at global poverty. The most accurate and up to date picture that we can get of global poverty is based on satellite data (in this case we will study the satellite image that relates the LandScan 2004 population count to the average digital number of DMSP satellite F15 nighttime lights at a specific location). In layman's terms this means that one has to measure the intensity of lights at specific locations that illuminate life on Earth and next to divide that light intensity by the number of people living at that location. Night illumination strongly correlates with economic activity.

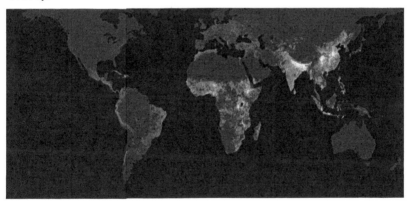

Source: Elvidge et al. (2009), Figure 2, p. 1654

Figure 6.3 Earth's poverty pockets (2004)

Economic activity per se, however, does not mean a lot. If many people live together the activity will be high even if these people are poor. Therefore it is the ratio of energy use (as exemplified by light intensity) to the population density that provides information on the incidence of poverty. The bright spots in Figure 6.3 represent Earth's poverty pockets and their geography as far as we can observe these accurately from space.

Lorenz Curve and Gini Coefficient

At a more abstract level Figure 6.4 summarizes recent data for Earth's income distribution by means of a so-called Lorenz curve. A Lorenz curve is a graph representing the cumulative distribution of a variable (in this case income). In Figure 6.4, horizontally the share of Earth population is shown. Vertically we can read the share in Earth income. For example Figure 6.4 shows that 40 per cent of Earth population earns only 5 per cent of Earth income. Earth would be on the 45° line if the world's income distribution would be perfectly equitable (in the sense that each earthling earns the same income). The data show a movement towards a more equitable (or better: less unfair) income distribution since the 1990s as the curve becomes a little bit flatter between 1990 and 2007.

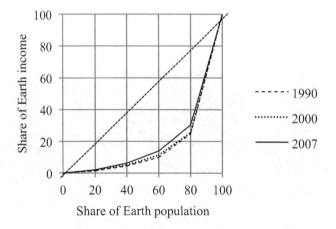

Source: Ortiz and Cummins (2011), Table 5 (PPP and constant dollars)

Figure 6.4   Lorenz curve (approximate planet income distribution by quintiles (1990 – 2007)

A useful measure of inequality in general is the so-called Gini-coefficient that essentially expresses the extent of deviation from the 45° line that signals perfect equality. In the theoretical case of perfect equality, the Gini-coefficient could be zero and express perfect equality if all earthlings would earn the same income. At the other theoretical extreme a Gini-coefficient of 1 would represent perfect inequality in the sense that one earthling earns the full Earth income and the other earthlings earn nothing at all.

Exercise 6.3 Inequality
- Approximate the Planet Gini coefficient by estimating the area above the Lorenz curve in per cent of the area below the 45° line.

While encouraging in itself the improvement between 1990 and 2007 in Figure 6.4 is a small step only in the direction of a more equitable global income distribution. Actually, the improvement that is illustrated in Figure 6.4 should be put into the long-run context that is developed in Figure 6.5 for the period 1820 – 2002. During the last two centuries global inequality has shown an almost constant trend towards greater inequality, although the evidence for the 1980s and 1990s according to Sali-I-Martin (2002) points to an improvement *vis-à-vis* the 1970s.

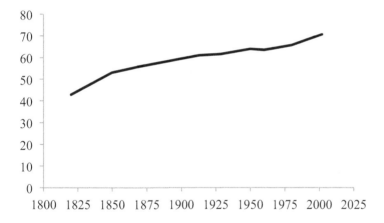

Figure 6.5   *Global Gini-coefficients (1820 – 2002) in per cent according to Milanovich (2009)*

The Globally Super Rich

Figure 6.6 provides yet another view on inequality. Now the focus is not on poverty (as in Figure 6.3) or on the equity of the distribution (Figures 6.4 and 6.5) but on the share of the globally super rich. The globally super rich are individuals that earn more that 20 times the average world income (in 2011 an individual was globally super rich if her income exceeded $222,000). Figure 6.6 shows that the fraction of the globally super rich in GPP decreased in the first half of the twentieth century and stabilized afterwards. This is yet another example of aggregate movements in the data that result from global shifts in norms and values. After the Second World War super richness became more exceptional (also because the living standards of ordinary people increased).

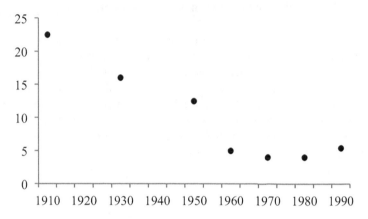

Source: Atkinson et al. (2011), Figure 4, p. 11.

Figure 6.6   Globally super rich (per cent of GPP, 1910 – 1990)

It is important to note that the presented global data series end before the new millennium. Recent trends in global inequality and poverty rates are subject of much debate. Even so, it is noteworthy that the majority of the Millennium Development Goals will only be met by a very few of the least developed countries (Table 6.1).

Table 6.1 Least Developed Countries that (can) achieve MDGs

	Achieved	On Track	Total
Poverty	2	3	5
Universal primary education	2	0	2
Gender parity in primary education	9	11	20
Gender parity in secondary education	2	5	7
Under-five mortality	0	3	3
Safe drinking water	6	4	10
Access to sanitation	2	1	3

Source: Calculations based on Go and Quijada (2011), Table 1, p. 8

From the perspective of this chapter inequality and redistribution are relevant in as far as taxes and government expenditures (including subsidies and transfers) have a short-run eartheconomic impact that is not symmetric.

Exercise 6.4 Asymmetry of taxes and subsidies
Use the model in Section 6.2 with exogenous government expenditure and exogenous taxation
  •   Show that the impact of an exogenous tax reduction by –1 differs
         from an increase in exogenous government spending by +1.

6.4   DEBT DYNAMICS

Government debt brings in completely new items and dimensions into the analysis since a budget deficit (surplus) in year *t* will increase (decrease) the stock of public debt *B* registered at the end of year *t* so that $Deficit = \Delta B = B_t - B_{t-1}$. The budget deficit consists of a primary deficit $G - T$ and the interest payments on debt outstanding RB_{t-1}.

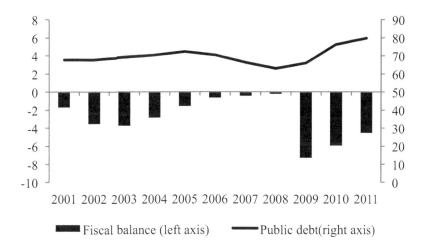

Source: IMF (2012) Figure 1.7

Figure 6.7   Earth's fiscal balance and public debt (2001 – 2011, per cent of GPP)

Therefore, we have for the full budget deficit $G + RB_{t-1} - T$ (if this expression is negative then the government runs a budget surplus as it spends less than it receives; in Figure 6.7 this is almost the case in 2007 and 2008).

A budget deficit will set debt dynamics into motion since we know that we have $B_t - B_{t-1} = G + RB_{t-1} - T$ or $B_t = G + (1+R) B_{t-1} - T$. This process is well illustrated in Figure 6.7 for the year 2009 and afterwards. As we saw in section 6.1 governments by and large cut taxes and/or increased spending in order to fight the Great Recession. The global fiscal balance moved from close to zero to minus seven per cent and the deficit continued to be substantial in 2010 and 2011 raising the public debt to GPP ratio from 63% to 80% in only three years.

Exercise 6.5 Debt dynamics
The following parameters can be derived from the IMF World Economic Outlook database: Nominal GPP in 2011 is 70 trillion and is expected to grow by 5.5% p.a. (see Exercise 3.5); the debt to GPP ratio in 2012 is 0.8 (Figure 6.7) and the government spending to GPP ratio is 0.15. The budget deficit is 4.5% Figure 6.7). The nominal interest rate is 4% (Figure 5.1). A tax to GPP ratio of 0.1375 could be consistent with these stylized facts.
- Calculate nominal GPP. Government expenditures, tax receipts and primary deficit for 2011 to 2017.
- Calculate interest payments, budget deficit and debt levels.
- Calculate the debt to GPP ratio and the budget deficit.
- What is your conclusion?
- Redo the calculations for interest payments, budget deficit and debt levels. First with an interest rate of 5%, then with a nominal GPP growth of 4.5% p.a.
- What is your conclusion?

6.5 KEY CONCEPTS

- Balanced budget multiplier
- Budget deficit
- Budget neutrality
- Budget surplus
- Fiscal stimulus
- Gini-coefficient
- Government spending

- Lorenz curve
- Lump sum tax
- Policy mix
- Progressive taxation
- Proportional taxation
- Public debt
- Stagflation

7. Money Matters! The LM Curve and Money Market Equilibrium

In January 2002, I received a shocking payment slip on which my salary was suddenly less than half the level of the previous month. The reason was not that I had done a bad job, but that the euro had been introduced overnight at a fixed exchange rate of 2.2 guilders to the euro. Fortunately for me, all prices of course also decreased by the same percentage. Therefore, if a car had cost 22,000 guilders before the introduction of the euro it would cost €10,000 after the introduction of the euro. Nothing had really changed because all prices were now also expressed in euro (and thus divided by 2.2) and the same was true for my mortgage and my saving account. Indeed, while my income was more than halved it did not matter because all prices (of goods and services and the factors of production) and the valuation of my debts and assets changed in the same way. The only thing that had changed was the amount of money that I had to keep in my purse. I always carried some 110 guilders in notes with me and this changed to 50 euro. My nominal money demand thus reduced from 110 to 50, but I could buy exactly the same amount of goods and services. If people do not suffer from money illusion, they will recognize these basic economic principles. An increase in the nominal value that is matched by the same increase in the general price level does not make a real change. In the long run people do not suffer from money illusion and this is why we will use the real money demand in our discussion.

But what is money? Money as we all know is what we and other people accept as a payment for goods and services and as a settlement of debts. Typically money performs three key functions: it is a medium of exchange, a unit of account and a store of value. Money is undifferentiated purchasing power: we can use it to pay for anything (it can be used in all exchanges). We use money to count and to compare prices. We can use money to save, that is: to delay consumption to a later moment in time. Not everything that performs these functions is legal tender, however. Legal tender is recognized by law or legal systems. In the 1970s when Italy experienced very high inflation a traveller in Rome would receive telephone coins and candy from the barrista as change and that could actually be saved and used to pay later for an espresso: medium of exchange, unit of account and store of value, but no legal tender. In the same vein the IMF's Special Drawing Rights are money, but Hub Culture's currency the Ven (www.hubculture.com) is not.

Text Box 7.1 Money aggregates

> The money stock is often reported for different aggregates. The most basic aggregate is M1 that consists of currency in circulation (notes and coins) and demand deposits and checks. These are the most liquid means of payment. The aggregate M2 consists of M1 to which has been added money market accounts and saving deposit accounts. These accounts are less liquid because one has to incur costs or wait before the money in the accounts can be withdrawn and used for payment. Definitions of higher aggregates differ over time and between countries depending on monetary strategy, stability of monetary relationships and market developments. At higher and thus less liquid levels bonds, treasuries and commercial paper may be added. This is near money as it requires markets to make the transformation from asset to M1 components.

7.1 MONEY DEMAND

The real money demand can be described as $L = L/P$ or as nominal money demand L divided by the general price level P. (L stands for liquidity; assets are considered more liquid if you can transform them more easily into money.) Money demand consists of three components based on precautionary motives (L_p), transaction motives (L_t) and speculative motives (L_s) with $L = L_p + L_t + L_s$.

Precautionary Demand

The real precautionary money demand ($l_p = l_{p0}$) is exogenous (that is, it is independent of Y and R) and reflects the human inclination to hold more cash in risky times. People want to keep more cash during uncertain times amongst others because they want to be fully liquid and prepared to act and move quickly in emergencies. Some observers have doubted that this motive still is valid in the current economic contexts, as it

> ... may be important only when no safe liquid asset other than money is available. In most advanced economies, however, the theory no longer applies because of the availability of short-term assets that pay a positive interest rate but pose no risk of capital losses (Sachs and Larrain, 1993, p. 240).

Typically, however, we can observe an increase in precautionary money demand during periods of economic crisis, social unrest and/or political and military conflicts. Also around the year 2000 precautionary demand increased because major '2K' problems were expected with computer systems as their codes were expected to be unable to handle the year '00'.

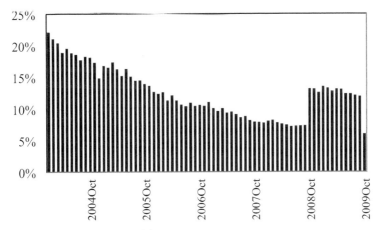

Source: ECB website www.ecb.int

Figure 7.1 Growth rate of Eurocurrency in circulation

Likewise during the first phase of the Great Recession this pattern occurred: Figure 7.1 shows that the growth rate of euro currency in circulation suddenly jumped in October 2008 when some of the major European banks had to be rescued by their governments. This kind of behaviour where people prefer cash and where they take their money from interest bearing accounts is called money hoarding.

Transaction Demand for Money

The transaction demand for money (also known as the real money balances) is also quite straightforward. If economic activity increases, we need more money to pay. Therefore we expect a positive relationship between the real transaction demand for money l_t and production so that $l_t = kY$ and $k > 0$ and the (nominal) demand for money balances $L_t = Pky$ or kY.

Transaction demand is related to a well-known macroeconomic expression, Fisher's velocity equation (the quantity theory of money): $MV = PT$, where M stands for the stock of money, V stands for the velocity with which this amount of money circulates, P stands for the general price level and *T* represents the number of transactions. If a hypothetical economy has to make 1000 transactions a year at a price of 2 then the money stock needs to be 2000 if the money does not circulate (for example when the transactions all take place at the end of the year). If the money circulates, less money is needed (for example when transactions take place on a quarterly basis the money stock needs to be 500 only). The product *PT* can at the macroeconomic level be equated to the national income so that we may also write $MV = Y$ or $M = {}^1/_V Y$ which resembles $L_t = Pky$ or kY.

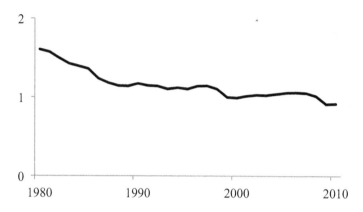

Sources: Calculations based on World DataBank and IMF World Economic Outlook database, April 2012

Figure 7.2 Global velocity (GPP/M2) 1980 – 2010

Figure 7.2 illustrates the development of velocity, which is quite stable after an initial decrease in the 1980s. The decrease in the 1980s may reflect the historical pattern of monetization of developing economies. Two smaller downward shifts are apparent following the Asian crisis in 1998 and the Great Recession, but the key message of Figure 7.2 is the relative stability over two decades.

Speculative Money Demand

The derivation of speculative money demand is a bit more complicated. This element of money demand is negatively related to the interest rate. One obvious reason for a negative relationship is that the opportunity costs of holding cash money (that is interest foregone) increase when the interest rate increases: people will put their money on saving accounts rather than keeping the cash. This simple observation provides a negative relationship, but this does not make the money demand speculative. For demand to be speculative, we need to have investors in bonds. Bonds essentially are special loan contracts. The issuer borrows from the holder (the lender) and has to pay interest at fixed intervals and repay the principal at the end of a pre-specified date (the maturity). For fixed interest rates, the interest payment will always be a fixed amount. A special bond is the perpetuity: a bond with no maturity (so the borrower only pays interest but never repays the principal). Now consider what happens with a perpetuity bond that pays 100 every year. How much would you value this bond? This of course depends on the general interest rate. If the interest rate were 10%, the bond would be worth 1000 to you. However, this price of the bond (its yield) may change of course: if the interest rate were 5%, you would value it at 2000. Therefore, if the interest rate is 10% and you expect that it will decrease you would be interested in buying the perpetuity now for 1000 and selling it later at a profit and realize the capital gain.

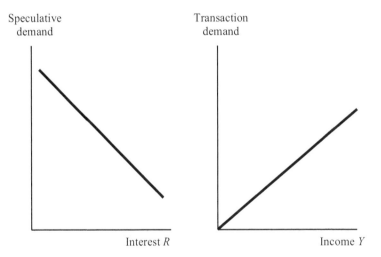

Speculative demand   Transaction demand

Interest *R*   Income *Y*

Diagram 7.1 Components of money demand

This is where speculation and money demand come in, since increasing your holding of bonds reduces your holding of money. Now if the interest rate for some reason is very low today most investors will expect a rise in interest and thus a reduction in the yield. In order to avoid a capital loss they will stick to cash. Therefore speculative money demand is highest at very low interest rates. Likewise, if the interest rate is considered 'unrealistically high' investors will go into bonds and speculative money demand is at its lowest. Therefore, we have a negative relationship between speculative money demand and the interest rate.

You will observe that the bond market is not modelled in the framework that we are developing. At the same time, however, the motivation for the curvature of the speculative money demand function clearly refers to bonds. Also when we discussed government we saw that the government can borrow (and it does so by issuing government bonds). So where are these bonds? Here the common practice is to rely on a principle from general equilibrium economics that allows us to eliminate one market. This principle is known as Walras' Law that states that if all 'other' $(n - 1)$ markets in the economy are in equilibrium then the nth market must by definition also be in equilibrium. Since we have product market equilibrium $(I = S)$ and money market equilibrium $(L = M)$ we thus know that the bond market must also be in equilibrium. Therefore economists most of the time do not model the bond market, also because in a financial market prices and quantities adjust quickly so that it is reasonable indeed to assume equilibrium in this market.

7.2   DERIVATION OF THE LM SCHEDULE

Next we write down an expression for total real money demand so that we have $l = l_p + l_t + l_s = kY - jR + l_{p0}$ and equate money demand to money supply M. The money supply is regulated by the Central Bank and we consider it to be an exogenous instrument variable, so $M = M_0$. Since we formulate money demand in real terms we also have to consider the real money stock M_0/P_0. Diagram 7.2 illustrates how an increase in the money stock from M_0 to M_1 reduces the interest rate R (movement on the money demand curve).

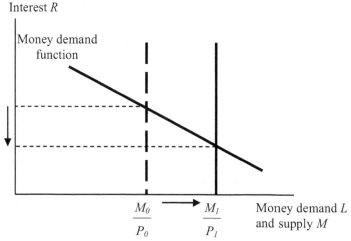

Diagram 7.2 An increase in the supply of money reduces the interest rate

Exercise 7.1 Money demand and money supply
- Check that the equilibrium in Diagram 7.2 is stable.
- Analyse the impact of an exogenous increase in speculative demand.
- Use diagram 7.2 to analyse what happens if Y increases.

We can plot the relationship between the income level and the interest rate in order to derive the $L = M$ (or simply LM) curve. This curve shows the combinations of Y and R for which we have macroeconomic equilibrium in the money market (Diagram 7.2). Starting from $L = M$ we can write the equilibrium condition as $M_0/P_0 = kY - jR + l_{p0}$ which we solve for R to obtain the expression for the LM curve $R = {}^k/_j Y + (l_{p0} - m_0)/j$ where $m_0 = M_0/P_0$. We draw the LM curve in (Y, R) space (see Diagram 7.3). The LM curve slopes upward since $k > 0$ and $j > 0$, but note that the LM curve can become vertical (if $j \downarrow 0$ or $k \rightarrow \infty$) or horizontal (if $k \downarrow 0$ or $j \rightarrow \infty$).

Interest R

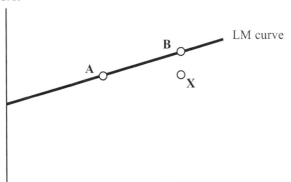

Diagram 7.3 The LM curve

Exercise 7.2 The LM curve
- Check that the equilibrium in Diagram 7.3 is stable using point X as the point of departure.
- Under which conditions do you expect $j \downarrow 0$, $j \rightarrow \infty$, $k \downarrow 0$ and $k \rightarrow 1$, respectively?
- Assess which factors shift the LM curve and in what direction.

Diagram 7.4 graphically illustrates the relationships that build the LM curve. As before some of the quadrants in the diagram appear to be upside down, but note that I measure from the origin and all variables are positive (compare Diagram 5.3). In the North West quadrant we have speculative demand for money. Lower R yields higher l_s (moving to the left in the mirrored diagram). In the South East we have the transaction demand for money upside down: larger Y implies larger l_t. South West is the equality $M_0/P_0 = kY - jR + l_{p0}$ represented by a 45° line. As shown by the dotted lines the LM curve represents combinations of R and Y where we have equilibrium between the demand for money and the money supply.

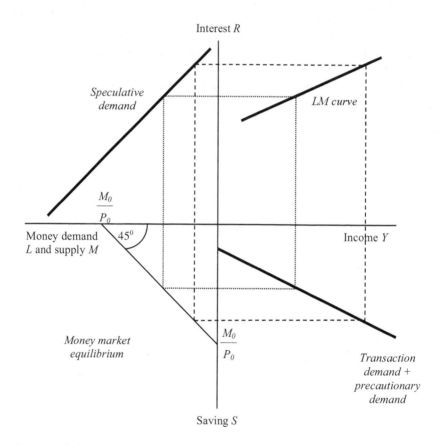

Diagram 7.4 Graphical derivation of the LM curve

Exercise 7.3 Shifting the LM curve
- Why does the South West quadrant of Diagram 7.4 represent money market equilibrium?
- Identify precautionary demand for money in Diagram 7.4.
- Use Diagram 7.4 to analyse the impact of an autonomous increase in the price level.

7.3 MONETARY POLICY AND THE GREAT RECESSION

Central banks have many instruments to steer the development of the money stock including reserve requirements, open market operations (when the central bank sells or buys government paper) and the official interest rates at which the central bank either lends or accepts deposits from commercial banks. In practice a combination of these instruments will be used, but for our analysis it does not really matter by which channel the central bank is influencing the economy. An increase in the money stock and a decrease in the official lending rates after all both reduce the interest rate that consumers and firms have to pay. It is this basic mechanism that we will incorporate in our model.

Text Box 7.2 The role of private banks: the money multiplier

Private banks create money when they lend more than savers deposit. Every time a bank lends the money supply increases. Since money creation is a profitable business and in order to protect depositors a check is put on the banking system: banks are required to hold a minimum fraction of deposits in reserve (the so called reserve requirements) defined as the reserve requirement ratio (ρ). Banks may choose to hold excess reserves and hold an extra fraction e of deposits held in reserve above and beyond the minimum requirement, for example, because they engage in risky activities or because they want to signal soundness and reliability.

Define the monetary base MB as $MB = C$ (currency in circulation) $+ R$ (bank reserves). Assume that the desired level of currency in circulation C in the economy is a constant fraction c of deposits D so that C changes in constant proportion to D. The Required Reserves RR equal ρD and the Excess Reserves are eD. The monetary base consists of required reserves, excess reserves, and currency in circulation: $MB = \rho D + eD + cD$ so that $MB = (\rho + e + c)D$. Rearrange: $D = MB/(\rho + e + c)$ and use $M1 = C + D$ (see Text Box 7.1).

The money multiplier can now be written as

$$M1 = \frac{1 + c}{\rho + e + c} MB$$

A larger multiplier means that banks create more money through lending and therefore the money supply will increase. The money multiplier increases due to smaller reserve requirements (set by the central bank), smaller excess reserves (reflecting bank policies) and smaller c (reflecting that the public wants to hold less cash *vis-à-vis* deposits).

Figures 7.3 and 7.4 provide a rough picture of the current stance of Earth's monetary policy. Monetary policy is either expansionary (other adjectives are lax and accommodating) or contractionary (strict). Figure 7.3 shows the development of the average global policy rate. Since 2009 the global policy rate reflects the unprecedented low official policy rates in the major developed economies. The central banks of these countries and monetary union have reduced their official rates in response to the financial and economic crisis. Since 2009 the US and Japan have no further scope for reducing the policy rate as they are actually at the zero rate floor. The euro policy rate was ¾ per cent only and although it could be reduced, the impact of that reduction would be minimal.

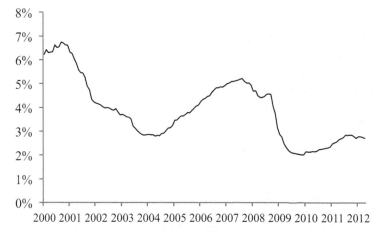

Sources: Monetary policy rates from http://www.centralbanknews.info/ and GDP
               weights from IMF World Economic Outlook Database, April 2012

*Figure 7.3   Global (production weighted) monetary policy rate (2000 – April
              2012)*

Since the interest rate could not be reduced by the usual instruments, central banks resorted to quantitative easing. Quantitative easing is a euphemism for printing money. Incidentally the number of notes in circulation does not change, the money is created electronically out of nothing and put on a central bank account. This account is used to buy financial assets from banks and other financial institutions (thus also serving the purpose of relieving them from some less liquid financial assets). Consequently central bank balance sheets expanded in several waves of quantitative easing, as illustrated in Figure 7.3.

Exercise 7.4 Monetary policy stance in the Great Recession
- What does Figure 7.3 imply for speculative demand?
- Determine the reduced form equation for Y, setting R at 0.
- What is the multiplier of Y with respect to M in this case?

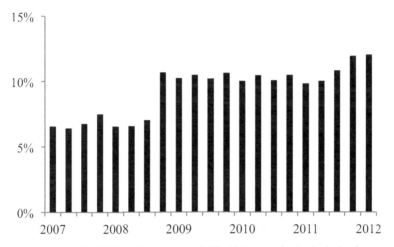

Sources: IMF (2012), Figure 1.5 and World Economic Outlook database, April 2012

Notes: Major central banks are Bank of Japan, ECB and FED

Calculations at current exchange rates and prices

Quarterly end of period data for central bank balance sheets are calculated in per cent of a quarter of annual GPP data

Figure 7.4   Quantitative easing (Major central bank balance sheets in per cent of GPP, end of period 2007 – 2012Q1)

There are many and yet unresolved issues regarding the monetary policy stance during the Great Recession. Since inflation does not really seem to be picking up, one might want to argue that the money creation episodes of quantitative easing have not posed serious risks to the world economy. In the same vein the low levels of the policy rates could have been at the appropriate level and these argumentations admittedly seem to have some validity (at least at the level of the countries that have decided to use these exceptional instruments). It is, however, much too early to come up with a more final analysis of these important policy issues at the global level. It is simply premature to assess whether monetary policy has been appropriate for the planet.

7.4 KEY CONCEPTS

- Bond
- Capital gain
- Excess reserves
- Fisher's velocity equation
- Hoarding
- Legal tender
- Liquidity
- M1, M2
- Maturity
- Monetary base
- Money illusion
- Money multiplier
- Money stock
- Open market operations
- Opportunity costs
- Perpetuity
- Precautionary money demand
- Quantitative easing
- Real money balances
- Reserve requirements
- Speculative money demand
- Transaction demand for money
- Velocity
- Walras' Law
- Yield

8. Eartheconomic Demand and Supply

This chapter brings together the building blocks that were developed in the previous chapters and combines the IS curve (equilibrium in the market for goods and services) and the LM curve (equilibrium in the money market) in order to arrive at a relationship between the general price level and the level of production for which the two markets are both simultaneously in equilibrium. This relationship describes how eartheconomic demand responds to the general price level. Next we develop the eartheconomic supply schedule (Section 8.3) and combine it with the demand side in Section 8.4 (see Diagram 8.1).

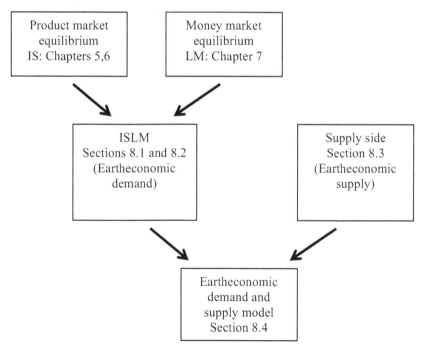

Diagram 8.1 Construction of the eartheconomic demand and supply model

8.1   DEMAND SIDE EQUILIBRIUM: I=S AND L=M

Now that we have studied product market equilibrium (I=S) and money market equilibrium (L=M) we can move on and see what it means if the economy meets these requirements simultaneously. Consider Diagram 8.2 which shows the IS curve and the LM curve in (y, R) space. In point E we have both product market equilibrium (point E is on the IS curve) and money market equilibrium (point E is on the LM curve).

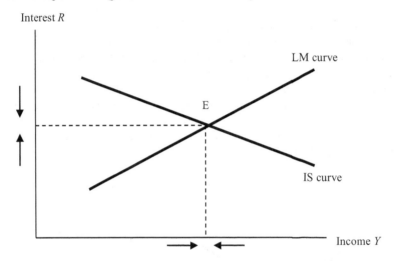

Diagram 8.2   Product market equilibrium and money market equilibrium in the ISLM model

The first thing to do is to check if this is a stable equilibrium. Points to the right (left) of the IS curve are characterized by a situation in which investment exceeds (is less than) planned investment so that inventories increase above (decrease below) desired levels and firms cut (increase) their production. Points above (below) the LM curve are characterized by excess supply of (demand for) money and this drives down (up) the interest rate. The equilibrium is thus stable.

Exercise 8.1 Excess money supply
* Explain why a point above the LM curve is characterized by excess supply of money.

Now let's check what happens if the IS curve shifts because government expenditures increase from G_0 to G_1. As illustrated in Diagram 8.3 this shifts the IS curve. The new curve IS(G_1) is to the right of the original curve IS(G_0) and the economy moves from E_0 (the original equilibrium) to E'. Point E', however, is not an equilibrium because there is an excess demand for money. The excess demand for money drives up the interest rate and when R starts to increase the economy moves along the new IS curve because the interest rate increase reduces investment and thus income. In this way the economy reaches the new equilibrium E_1. It follows from our discussion that this equilibrium is characterized by both a higher level of G (the original impulse) and a higher interest rate R. Since R increased, it follows that speculative demand l_s and investment I must be lower in E_1 than in E_0. Income Y has increased, but by less than in the case that we analysed in Chapter 5. This implies that the government spending multiplier is lower due to the fact that the interest rate increase reduces investment. So in this case investment is partially crowded out by government spending. Since income increases from E_0 to E_1 we also know that transaction demand increased (actually, since M has not changed by implication transaction demand increased as much as speculative demand decreased).

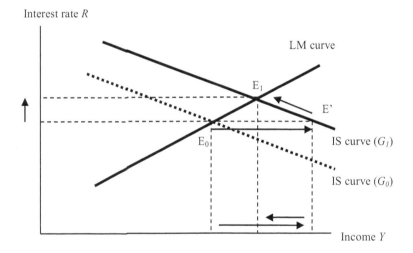

Diagram 8.3 An increase in government spending in the ISLM model

Our model has become more complicated again and it pays to carefully check if the model is determined. One easy pre-flight check is to count the number of endogenous variables. You need as many equations as you have endogenous variables in order to be able to solve the model. If you have more equations than endogenous variables, the model is over determined. If you have fewer equations than endogenous variables, you cannot solve the model.

Consumption function:	$C_t = cY + C_0$	(8.1)
Definition equation:	$S = Y - C$	(8.2)
Investment function:	$I = I_0 - iR$	(8.3)
Government spending function:	$G = G_0$	(8.4)
Tax function:	$T = T_0$	(8.5)
Definition equation:	$l = l_p + l_t + l_s$	(8.6)
Real precautionary money demand function:	$l_p = l_{p0}$	(8.7)
Real transaction money demand function:	$l_t = kY$	(8.8)
Real speculative money demand function	$l_s = -jR$	(8.9)
Equilibrium equation (money market):	$M_0/P_0 = l$	(8.10)
Equilibrium equation (product market):	$I + G = S + T$	(8.11)

Endogenous: $Y, C, I, S, G, T, R, l, l_p, l_t$ and l_s
Exogenous: $c, r, I_0, C_0, G_0, T_0, P_0, M_0, j, k$ and l_{p0}

We have several ways to solve this model. A first solution is to equate IS and LM.

IS is:
$$R = \frac{C_0 + I_0 + G_0 - cT_0}{i} - \frac{(1-c)}{i}Y \tag{8.12}$$

LM is:
$$R = \frac{k}{j}Y + \frac{l_{p0} - \frac{M_0}{P_0}}{j} \tag{8.13}$$

At the intersection of IS and LM we have of course the same R on the curves and from this we calculate the reduced form equation of Y as:

$$Y = \frac{\dfrac{\frac{M_0}{P_0} - l_{p0}}{j} + \dfrac{C_0 + I_0 + G_0 - cT_0}{i}}{\dfrac{k}{j} + \dfrac{(1-c)}{i}} \tag{8.14}$$

Exercise 8.2 Reduced form equations in the ISLM model
Using different routes provides an antidote against errors.
- Use $I + G = S + T$ to determine the reduced form equation for Y.
- Use $L = M$ to determine the reduced form equation for Y.
- Use $Y = C + I + G$ to determine the reduced form equation for Y.

Also do not forget to check that a reduced form equation consists of exogenous variables only and check the plausibility of the signs of the multipliers. For example, government expenditure, money supply and the autonomous components of consumption and investment have a positive multiplier; taxes have a negative multiplier.

8.2   EARTHECONOMIC DEMAND

The reduced form equation again enables us to figure out how income reacts to changes in the exogenous variables. For example, you can directly see and check from equation 8.14 that an increase in the price level P_0 will induce a decrease of Y. This gives us an important eartheconomic relationship: the eartheconomic demand function (see Diagram 8.4). You can also observe how policy instruments work out: you can stimulate macroeconomic demand (increase Y) by increasing the money supply and/or government spending and by reducing taxation (it should be clear that the use of these policy instruments represent shifts of the LM curve and the IS curve, respectively, to the right in Diagram 8.3; note that the macroeconomic demand function in Diagram 8.4 shifts in the same direction).

Exercise 8.3 Eartheconomic demand
- Explain why the IS (LM) curve and the eartheconomic demand curve shift in the same direction.

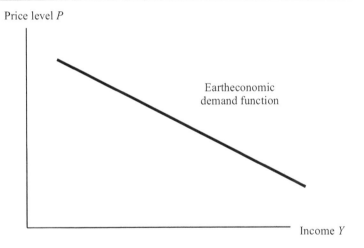

Diagram 8.4 Eartheconomic demand schedule

Demand Management during the Great Recession

Now let us consider the 2009 fiscal and monetary policy responses to the Great Recession. The starting point is that eartheconomic demand decreased on several accounts as we have already seen in previous chapters: the decrease in investment has been illustrated in Figures 2.1, 4.1 and 5.2. Figure

7.1 indicated an increase in precautionary money demand. It is therefore also likely that exogenous consumption decreased at that time.

Exercise 8.4 Eartheconomic demand and the Great Recession
- Check in the reduced form equation 8.14 that these factors shift the eartheconomic demand schedule to the left.

Next consider policy responses around the globe that as documented in Figure 6.1 almost universally consisted of fiscal and monetary stimulus. The global policy change is documented in Figure 6.7 (fiscal policy), Figure 7.3 (monetary policy rates) and Figure 7.4 (quantitative easing). This is how the ISLM framework can be used to tell this story of a drop in demand and the response by larger government expenditures (and or/lower taxes) and accommodating monetary policy. In Diagram 8.5 the point of departure is the equilibrium E_0 at the intersection of the original LM curve (LM_0) and IS curve (IS_0). The drop in demand (investment and/or consumption) shifts the IS curve down to IS_1 and the new equilibrium is E_1 on the original LM curve. Monetary policy alone shifts the LM curve out to LM_{0+M}; fiscal policy alone shifts the IS curve out to IS_{1+F}; the combination of monetary and fiscal policy shifts both curves out and results in a new equilibrium E_{F+M}.

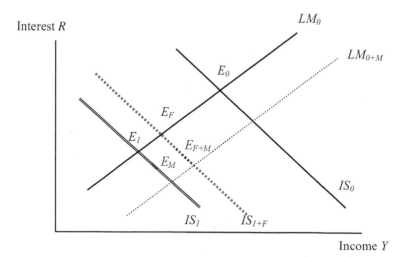

Diagram 8.5 Demand contraction followed by expansionary fiscal and monetary policy

Exercise 8.5 Shifting curves
- Explain why point E_F must be 'higher' than point E_M.
- Use an ISLM diagram to illustrate how monetary and fiscal policy can respond to an increase in precautionary money demand.

It is important to realise that macroeconomic demand cannot be analysed in isolation of the supply side of the economy. For example, an increase in demand cannot be met if the economy is already at its full employment level, so that all factors of production are used to the full in the production process. As illustrated in Diagram 8.6 a tax cut will in the case of full employment increase demand, but not supply and therefore the only way out is an increase in the price level. Inflation means that the real money stock decreases (the nominal money stock does by assumption not change) so R goes up and investment is reduced. Actually, in this case government expenditure fully crowds out investment.

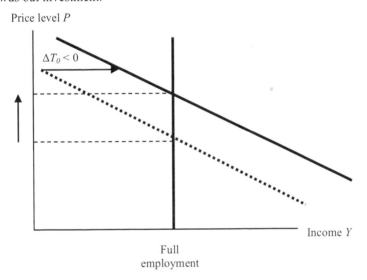

Diagram 8.6 Tax cut at full employment

The examples in Diagram 8.5 and 8.6 clearly illustrate that the impact and effectiveness of macroeconomic demand management depend on prevalent conditions of time and place (we will return to this issue in Chapter 9). It is yet another way of saying that both sensible analysis and sensible policy need to take the demand and supply conditions simultaneously into consideration.

8.3   EARTHECONOMIC SUPPLY

Eartheconomic supply in our model is produced by combining labour L and capital K in the production process. People work with tools, machines and infrastructures build in the past. (One could of course add other factors such as nature or energy and while that would be more realistic it would also complicate the analysis unnecessarily.) All these capital goods are the result of investments in earlier years; in this Part we are not concerned with the production capacity generating aspect of investment; we will take this up in Part II. Basically, the stock of capital is available at the beginning of the period of analysis and the question is how and to what extent this stock will be used in combination with the available amount of labour.

The production function describes how combinations of K and L are used to create production Q so that we have $Q = Q \, (K, \, L)$. Essentially two archetypes of production functions can be distinguished. On the one hand we have the production schemes that require minimal fixed amounts of both K and L for each level of output (an example is the Harrod-Domar production function with fixed technical coefficients that we will discuss in Chapter 10). These production schemes tell us that capital and labour will be used in fixed amounts. A carpenter for example will not increase his production if he gets a second hammer, and likewise 10 carpenters with only 1 hammer at their disposal will produce considerably less than if each of them had a hammer. On the other hand we have the production functions that allow for some substitution (the Solow model to be discussed in Chapter 10 is an example). Machines can replace employees to some extent; more employees can sometimes achieve similar production as could be produced with more capital.

In the case of substitution different quantities of labour and capital can thus be combined to reach a particular level of production. Firms make the decision on the mix of production factors on the basis of their contribution to the production (capital productivity and labour productivity, respectively) and compare these benefits to the costs of the factors of production (the rental cost of capital and the wage rate, respectively). If the wage rate increases firms will tend to invest in labour saving technologies reducing the amount of labour and increasing the amount of capital that is used in the production process.

Typically, substitution implies reallocation of the factors of production and that requires time (building machines, hiring and firing of employees). So often in the short term the possibilities for substitution are rather limited and the production scheme might look more like the fixed technical coefficient scheme. The two archetypes are illustrated in Diagram 8.7 that shows so-called isoquants (combinations of K and L that yield the same level of output). Note that the production level Q_1 must exceed Q_0 because larger amounts for the factor of production are used for Q_1.

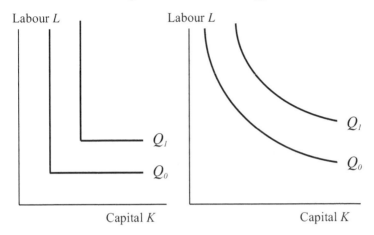

Diagram 8.7 Isoquants without (left) and with (right) substitution

We can also express the information contained in the isoquants in Diagram 8.7 by the production function that relates labour to production for fixed amounts of capital. The solid lines in Diagram 8.8 show production levels for different amounts of labour. The dotted lines show what happens if the amount of capital increases due to investment (similar shifts occur if the efficiency of the production process and/or the production technology improve). In the absence of substitution the minimum level of labour necessary to produce the output is the amount of labour demanded.

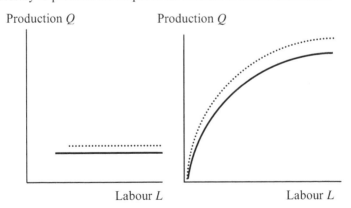

Diagram 8.8   Production functions with fixed technical coefficients (left) and substitution (right)

Demand and Supply of Labour

Now let us move to the labour market as one of the abstract markets where eartheconomic supply is determined. In Chapter 3 (Figures 3.7 and 3.8) we observed fluctuations in unemployment (so where labour supply exceeds labour demand for the Earth economy). Some of the unemployment is frictional, as when people are in between jobs and some unemployment is seasonal (ice cream shops are out of business during winter). These sources of unemployment can be important, but not of concern to us in this book as the unemployment level is not related to fluctuations in eartheconomic demand. So how do demand and supply of labour interact?

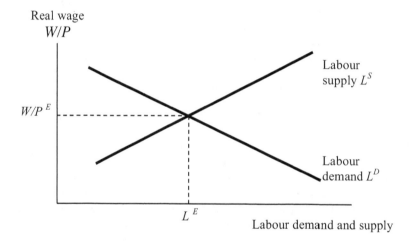

Diagram 8.9 Labour market (neoclassical)

Labour supply L^S is determined by households who balance the benefits of free time (leisure) against the wage that can be earned (the amount of goods and services that can be consumed). Typically the higher the real wage rate W/P, the larger the supply of labour so that we have $L^S = L^S(W/P)$ and $L^{S'} > 0$. Therefore the labour supply function in Diagram 8.9 is upward sloping. (Note, however, that this general pattern may not be valid at low or below subsistence levels, where a reduction in the wage rate could actually induce more labour supply simply to be able to earn the income necessary to survive.) Labour demand L^D is determined by firms. Firms maximize profits and will hire more labour as long as the real wage rate exceeds the marginal product of labour (the productivity of the last employee hired). If the real wage rate rises firms will cut back employment so labour demand $L^D =$

$L^D(W/P)$ is downward sloping ($L^{D'} < 0$). The equilibrium wage rate W/P^E yields the full employment equilibrium quantity of employed labour L^E and using the production function we find the full employment eartheconomic production level $Q^E = Q(K, L^E)$.

Exercise 8.6 Labour market
- Check the stability of the labour market equilibrium in Diagram 8.9.
- What factors shift the labour demand curve?
- What factors shift the labour supply curve?

Unemployment and Output Gap

The neoclassical interpretation of our labour market model is straightforward. If eartheconomic demand reduces, then the real wage will immediately adjust so that supply equals demand and no unemployment occurs. It is possible to get unemployment in the neoclassical world but only when distortions are introduced. Let us assume that a wage level has been set above the market clearing level, for example, because a minimum wage level has been set by the government or negotiated by trade unions. (This wage level is indicated by an asterisk * in Diagram 8.10.) At this wage level labour supply L^{S*} exceeds labour demand L^{D*} so there is unemployment $U = L^{S*} - L^{D*}$ and when we translate this with the aid of the production function we find an output gap (actual output is smaller than potential output). Distortions of the market process can thus explain the occurrence of unemployment and output gaps. An important eartheconomic observation, however, is the world output gap $(Y - Y^E) / Y^E$ is fluctuating as illustrated in Figure 8.1.

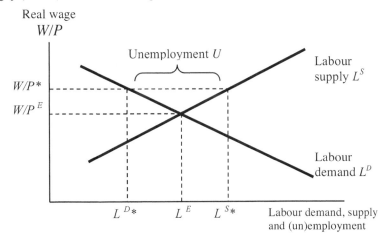

Diagram 8.10 Labour market with minimum wage

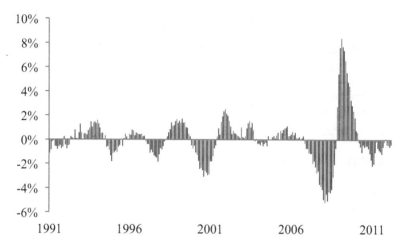

Notes: Monthly data for industrial production. Potential output determined with
                a HP filter with λ = 14400
Source: Calculations based on CPB world trade monitor

Figure 8.1a Earth output gap (1991 – March 2012, in per cent)

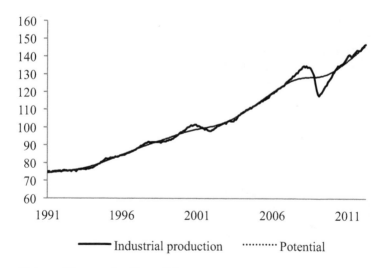

Notes and Source: See Figure 8.1a

*Figure 8.1b World industrial production and potential world industrial
production (index numbers, 1991 – March 2012)*

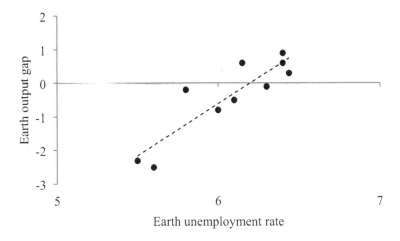

Note: Excludes data point for 2009 (output gap −5.2%, unemployment 6.2%)
Sources: See Figures 3.7 and 8.1

Figure 8.2 Okun's Law: Earth output gap and unemployment rate in per cent, 2001 – 2011)

The relationship between fluctuations in the world output gap and world unemployment (also known as Okun's Law) is illustrated in Figure 8.2. The relationship at the planetary level is in line with this empirical regulation that was first observed by Okun (1962) at the national level. Okun's Law can be written as $(Y - Y^E) / Y^E = \beta (U - U^*)$ with U^* the natural (or structural) rate of unemployment. Historically, the coefficient β is about 3, as in Figure 8.2 (but also note that this figure excludes the observation for the year 2009).

Exercise 8.7 Okun's Law
- Check the size of the coefficient β in Figure 8.2.

One practical way out to both salvage the neoclassical approach and explain the occurrence of short-term fluctuations is to argue that the neoclassical model describes the long run while an upward-sloping supply function deals with the short term. The Keynesian supply schedule becomes neoclassical so to speak at the point where eartheconomic demand equals the full employment production level.

Long-Run Supply

Long-run eartheconomic supply is represented by a vertical line (Diagram 8.11). The location of the supply function is determined by the quality and quantity of the available factors of production. In the long run the price level does not matter for the level of production, because production that exceeds long-run supply will ultimately create a price reduction and production below the long-run level increases prices eventually inducing an increase in supply. In the end the economy will therefore return to the long-run equilibrium. Some economists even argue that prices will adjust so quickly that convergence to long-run supply will almost be immediate.

Other factors than prices can, however, influence the location of the eartheconomic supply function. The supply curve shifts in (to the left) when the quality and/or quantity of the factors of production decrease. Examples of inward shifting factors are: disasters and wars, but also the process of creative destruction can lead to an inward shift if well established technologies and knowledge become obsolete. The replacement of sailing by the steam engine and the consecutive replacement of steam by the combustion engine are examples of creative destruction. Likewise outward shifts (to the right) occur if the quantity and/or quality of Earth's production factors increases. Examples of such factors are: population increases, technological progress, increases in (human) capital and discoveries of national resources. Also policy shifts can exert a positive or negative influence: a more vigorous competition policy would enhance efficiency and would *ceteris paribus* increase Earth production.

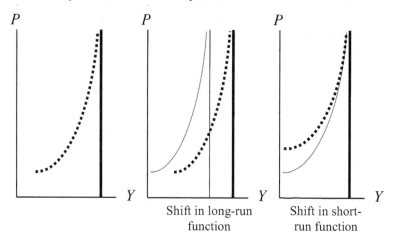

Diagram 8.11 Long-run and short-run production functions

Short-Run Supply

The short-term eartheconomic supply curve (the dotted line in Diagram 8.11) is upward sloping reflecting that deviations from the long-run equilibrium are possible, for example because price adjustment takes time or because prices are sticky. Short-term deviations from potential (or long-run) eartheconomic supply are then possible. The short-term supply function shifts up due to cost push inflation (increases in the prices of intermediate inputs, including energy, unit labour costs, and depreciation due to technological shifts) but also when direct taxation increases (Value Added Tax, border taxes). The short-term curve shifts down when wages are moderated and when subsidies reduce the general price level.

8.4   COMBINING EARTHECONOMIC SUPPLY AND DEMAND

The final step is to bring eartheconomic supply and eartheconomic demand into one model, that is to combine Diagram 8.4 (the downward sloping eartheconomic demand curve) and Diagram 8.11 (the short-run and long-run macroeconomic supply curve). Diagram 8.12 thus presents the full model of the Earth economy. Underlying the eartheconomic demand and eartheconomic supply functions are on the demand side the ISLM model (that is: the money and product markets of the economy) and on the supply side the labour market. (Walras' Law, as discussed earlier, has eliminated the bond market.)

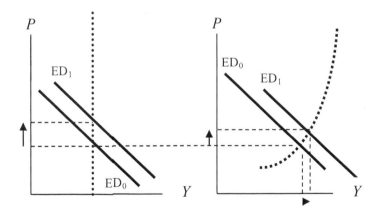

Diagram 8.12   Eartheconomic demand and long-run/short-run supply

Diagram 8.12 illustrates how demand and supply interact in the case of an increase in eartheconomic demand from ED_0 to ED_1. Confronted with the long-run production function (so when the economy is at full capacity) this increase in demand has but one outlet: higher prices. The short-run supply curve is relevant when there is spare capacity. Also here we have an increase in price (but smaller) and in contrast to the left-hand panel of Diagram 8.12, the right-hand panel shows a movement of production towards the full employment production level.

Exercise 8.8 Eartheconomic demand and supply
- Analyse how a decrease in long-run supply (the function shifts to the left) impacts on price and output. Do this for the two options depicted in Diagram 8.12.

8.5   KEY CONCEPTS

- Fixed technical coefficients
- Frictional unemployment
- Isoquant
- Marginal product
- Okun's law
- Output gap
- Potential production

- Production function
- Real wage
- Rental cost of capital
- Seasonal unemployment
- Structural unemployment
- Substitution

9. Puzzling Disagreements

Economists disagree a lot. Winston Churchill observed once: 'If you put two economists in a room, you get two distinct opinions, unless one of them is Lord Keynes, in which case you get three opinions'. Most of the time the disagreement amongst economists is about the value of the parameters of the model. Many discussions between economists can be related to their point of reference regarding the curvature of the IS and LM curves and their location *vis-à-vis* the long-run macroeconomic supply functions. So in a debate we can find Monetarists to be somewhere on the right-hand part of the LM curve while Keynesians are more on the left-hand segment. Both can be right, but not at the same time! The Monetarist school was probably right in the 1980s; the Keynesian recipe became the tune of the day during the initial responses to the financial and economic crisis that started in 2007. Indeed, the validity of a theory depends on conditions of time and place. Experienced economists recognize that the parameters are not fixed for eternity, but critically depend on conditions of time and place. The upshot is that a particular version of a model or a theory may be appropriate for a particular country or for a particular period in time. But once conditions change, as they ultimately always do, a different version may become more relevant.

A second reason why economists may disagree is because they have different time horizons in mind when they formulate their hypotheses or their claims. For example, in the very short term one can perhaps ignore the fact that an increase in government spending causes a larger public debt, but in the long run it is obviously unavoidable to take this change into account. Often the disagreement of economists is puzzling, but can be reconciled by finding out about what parameters they actually disagree on and then find out by empirical research who is 'right' (at this moment and this place of course). In this chapter we will try to find solutions to some of the puzzles.

9.1   INTEREST RATE SENSITIVITY OF THE IS CURVE

Consider by way of example Diagram 9.1 that shows a vertical IS curve signifying that the IS curve is interest rate insensitive (so by implication consumption, investment and government spending are not influenced by

changes in the interest rate). This particular assumption about a key
parameter (the interest rate sensitivities or elasticities of consumption,
investment and government expenditures, respectively) has major
implications for policy analysis. The left hand panel shows the starting point.
In the middle panel the LM curve shifts (for example, because the central
bank increases the money supply) but with no real economy effect (the
interest rate decreases, but this has no impact on spending). The right hand
panel of Diagram 9.1 shows that fiscal policy is effective in this case. Fiscal
policy shifts the IS curve outwards (to the right) increasing both national
income Y and the interest rate R. Hence when the components of effective
demand (consumption, investment and government expenditures) on balance
are interest insensitive monetary policy is ineffective while fiscal policy is
effective. This is essentially the simple model that we discussed in Chapter 4,
but this time with a money market included in the model. There are several
stories that can be told in the context of Diagram 9.1. For example, another
way to tell the story of the middle diagram is to argue that increasing the
money supply does reduce the interest rate, but that the increase in supply is
fully absorbed by an increase in speculative demand. Typically assumptions
about the shape and locus of the curve explain why economists differ on their
views on the (in)effectiveness of policy instruments.

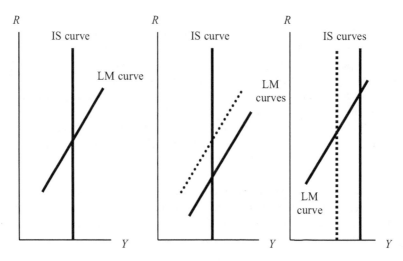

*Diagram 9.1 Monetary policy is ineffective and fiscal policy is effective if
the IS curve is interest insensitive*

Exercise 9.1 Interest rate sensitivity and the IS curve

Assume a perfectly elastic (horizontal) IS curve.

- What does perfectly elastic mean in this case?
- Analyse effectiveness of monetary and fiscal policies in this case.

It is important to note that Diagram 9.1 shows an extreme position only (namely perfect inelasticity of effective demand components) and although this provides a clear and transparent case it is more likely in ordinary discussions to find that the arguments of economists differ in degree rather than in the extremes. Thus a point of discussion would in the economic discourse probably be expressed in terms of the actual size and significance of the interest rate sensitivity of the IS curve. How could such a much more nuanced argument be framed? Diagram 9.2 tells that story with more nuances. The diagram illustrates that the same increase in money supply works out differently depending on the steepness and locus of the IS curve. The increase in the money supply shifts the LM curve out from LM_0 to LM_1 and this identical shift has quantitatively different consequences for the two IS curves in Diagram 9.2, namely for a relatively interest sensitive IS curve ($IS_{Sensitive}$) and for a relatively insensitive curve ($IS_{insensitive}$). The impact is qualitatively comparable (in both cases the interest rate decreases and national income increases) and the differences are not absolute as in Diagram 9.1 but differ in degree. It is, however, clear that the more interest rate sensitive the IS curve, the stronger the impact of monetary policy.

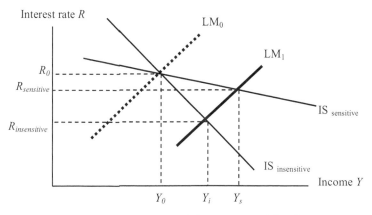

Diagram 9.2 Relative interest rate (in)sensitivity of the IS curve

Exercise 9.2 Interest rate sensitivity and the IS curve
- Explain why in Diagram 9.2 we find that $R_S > R_I$ and $Y_I < Y_S$.
- What does this imply for the different components of money demand?

9.2 INTEREST RATE SENSITIVITY OF THE LM CURVE

Specific assumptions have of course also been made regarding the locus and curvature of the LM curve. Diagram 9.3 shows in a stylized way that we may have two special sections at the begining and end of a LM curve (in addition to the middle section that has the usual upward sloping property). On the one hand we have an interest insensitive LM curve, that basically reflects that at very high levels of interest speculative balances will be reduced to zero (and then a further increase in R will have no influence, since obviously we have $l_S \geq 0$; your wallet can be empty but it is not a black hole).

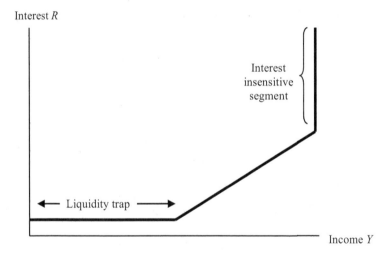

Diagram 9.3 Liquidity trap and interest insensitive segment of LM curve

On the other hand we have the so-called liquidity trap (a situation in which people become indifferent between holding money and bonds). In the interest insensitive part of the LM curve we are in the Monetarist's domain and money demand is governed simply by transaction demand. Some Monetarists have turned Fisher's quantity theory upside down and argue that money supply determines economic growth and that a constant growth rate of the money supply is therefore warranted. It is easy to see that fiscal policy is ineffective in the interest rate insensitive (vertical) part of the LM curve in

Diagram 9.3. An increase in government spending will raise the interest rate and this will yield an equal reduction in investment (another example of crowding out). The assumption of interest insensitivity of the LM curve is instrumental in the economic discourse since it helps to frame the Monetarist's priority for money supply as the steering mechanism of economic activity in the modern monetary economy.

Liquidity Trap

At the left-hand side of Diagram 9.3 we find the liquidity trap. Interestingly, some see the liquidity trap as a debating trick: Sachs and Larrain, (1993, p. 370) for example observe that the liquidity trap is an 'extreme case that was suggested by Keynes as having applicability during the Great Depression (but which is now viewed as mainly a theoretical curiosity)'. It is of course rather interesting that the conditions in the world economy in the Great Recession pretty much resemble the liquidity trap that Keynes (1936) envisaged in his *General Theory*.

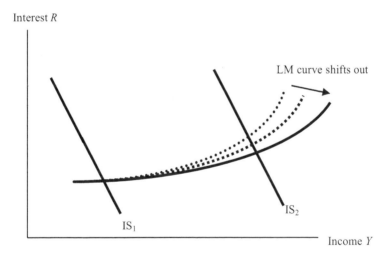

Diagram 9.4 A closer look at the liquidity trap

It is therefore useful to consider in somewhat more detail the liquidity trap in Diagram 9.4. The diagram shows by way of illustration two IS curves that represent low and high product market demand, respectively. The liquidity trap problem bites in the LM curvature: at the low end of the LM curve people are indifferent between holding money and holding bonds. An increase in money supply shifts the high end of the LM curve outwards but has no effect at the low end because it basically feeds speculative money holdings.

Exercise 9.3 Liquidity trap
- What factors could explain the different locations of the two IS curves in Diagram 9.4.
- Show that fiscal policy is the only effective government instrument in the liquidity trap.

Diagram 9.5 provides another perspective on the same issue that is of particular relevance to policy makers in the second phase of the Great Recession. A reduction in government expenditure (for example to restore fiscal sustainability) has a much bigger impact if the LM curve is flat (because in this case the multiplier is the simple Keynesian multiplier that we developed in Chapter 6). The message is sobering. It is not only fiscal stimulus that is more effective at the exceptionally low interest rate levels of the Great Recession; the same is true for austerity measures with clearer and larger risks for economic activity during crises. Turrini et al. (2012), for example, find that the growth impact of fiscal policy is four times stronger during a crisis than in normal times.

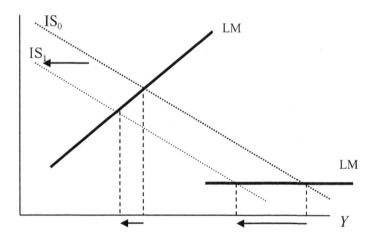

Diagram 9.5 Austerity measures have a stronger impact in the liquidity trap

9.3 DEMAND AND FULL EMPLOYMENT SUPPLY

Diagram 9.6 provides the ISLM model as developed in Section 8.1 but adds some crucial information to Diagram 8.2, namely the location of the full employment level Y^E. In the left hand panel of the diagram, the economy starts at the full employment level and an increase in demand (an outward shift of the IS curve) thus fully feeds into inflation. The rise in the price level P reduces real money supply (M/P) and increases the interest rate (the LM curve shifts inward to the left). Higher interest feeds negatively into investment that is crowded out by the increasing other demand component(s) that shifted the IS outward.

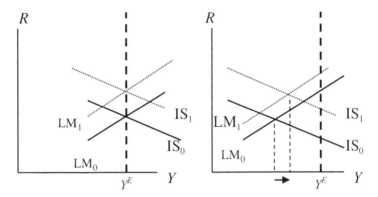

Diagram 9.6 ISLM and full employment level

Int the right hand panel of Diagram 9.6 the economy is below full employment and therefore the shift of the IS curve from IS_0 to IS_1 results in an increase in income Y. Also in this case the general price level increases due to higher demand but this time to a smaller extent so that the increase in the rate of interest is also more modest and investment is not fully crowded out.

Exercise 9.4 ISLM and full employment
- Why does the price level also increase in the case depicted by the right hand side of Diagram 9.6?
- Analyse how a reduction of the full employment level impacts on the IS and LM curve (the economy starts at full employment).

9.4 PRICE RIGIDITY

Economists also disagree a lot on the speed of price adjustment. At one side of the spectrum we have economists that see price adjustment as almost instantaneous. In this vision all changes in underlying costs, technology, preferences and scarcities are reflected in the market price and the market price moves freely. On the other side of the spectrum we have economists that observe that it is costly to change prices, for example due to menu costs (the costs to change listed prices), customer-supplier relationships (in which prices are agreed for longer periods and not subject to daily change) or a lack of competition. An intermediate group of economists argues that prices are rigid in the downward direction, pointing out for example that employees resist cuts in nominal wages or that firms are keen to pass cost increases to the consumer but like the windfall profit of cost reductions. Diagram 9.7 illustrates two extreme visions often presented as the archetypes of neoclassical versus Keynesian economics.

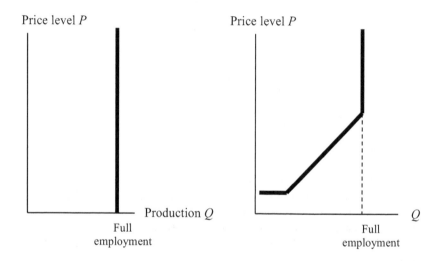

Diagram 9.7   Neoclassical (left) and Keynesian (right) eartheconomic supply curves

It is most instructive to concentrate on the right hand side schedule in Diagram 9.7. The Keynesian supply curve starts flat, because at very low levels of demand price increases are unlikely. After all, firms will have substantial spare capacity (and thus will not increase prices), while unemployment is high so that wages will be moderated.

Exercise 9.5 Price rigidity
- Analyse how a similar increase in government expenditure impacts on the price and output levels in the three segments of the Keynesian eartheconomic supply curve.

At some point the normal upward sloping short-term supply function takes prominence until the neoclassical vision becomes relevant at full employment. At that point stimulating fiscal policy and monetary policy will simply generate inflation. Consider Figure 9.1 that illustrates the relationship between money growth and inflation at the planetary level. The correlation is not particularly strong but still we see that growth rates of the money supply are associated with higher inflation giving credence to both Fischer's quantity theory and the idea that excessive money supply generates inflation.

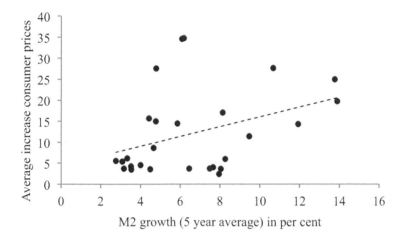

Sources: World DataBank and IMF World Economic Outlook April 2012 database

Figure 9.1 Earth money growth and inflation 1984 – 2010

9.5 IDENTIFICATION

From the previous sections it will have become clear that economists often differ about their theories and that theories may or may not be relevant for the economic context to which the analysis pertains. But why is it so difficult to distinguish which approach is the right one given the conditions of time and place that prevail? Consider Diagram 9.8. The diagram illustrates an observed movement from *A* to *B* representing a reduction in both the market interest rate *R* and income *Y*. The problem with this observation is that it is consistent both with a demand shock (the IS curve shifts in from IS_0 to IS_1) and with a supply shock (the full employment output level shifts to the left from Y^E_0 to Y^E_1. Importantly and unfortunately these different options give rise to completely different policy prescriptions. A demand shock could be

met by an increase of government expenditure and/or a more accommodating
monetary policy. If the problem, however, originates on the supply side of
the economy as in the right hand panel of Diagram 9.8, then those policies
would only increase inflation and public debt.

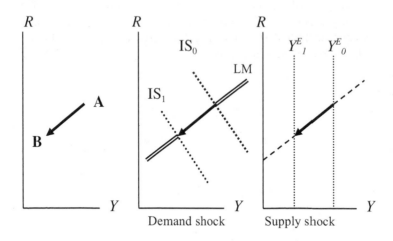

Diagram 9.8 Identification problems

Exercise 9.6 Identification
- Investigate potential underlying changes in ISLM and supply and
  demand schedules that could explain an increase in the interest rate
  R while income Y does not change.

9.6   KEY CONCEPTS

- Conditions of time and place
- Demand shock
- Downward rigidity
- Identification
- Interest rate sensitivity
- Keynesian economics
- Keynesian supply curve

- Liquidity trap
- Monetarists
- Neoclassical economics
- Neoclassical supply curve
- Price rigidity
- Supply shock

PART II

LONG RUN

10. Long-Run Growth

So far we have dealt with short-term fluctuations and the macroeconomic policies that we studied by and large were designed to stabilize the economy. In this chapter we take a look at the long run. We start with a graph that depicts the very long run indeed. Figure 8.1 is based on the pioneering historical statistics by Angus Maddison. The figure shows how GPP and the world population developed since the year '0'. Note that the time axis is not linear. It jumps in earlier periods because Maddison estimated production and population at appropriate moments in time. Essentially until the Middle Ages the world economy was stagnant in terms of the people that inhabited the Earth and their production. Here the underlying mechanism was that income was and remained at the survival level or slightly above. Only after the increases in productivity during the Industrial Revolution a substantial increase in the rates of growth of world population and GPP became possible.

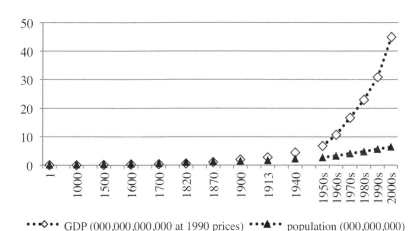

••◇•• GDP (000,000,000,000 at 1990 prices) ••▲•• population (000,000,000)

Source: Maddison's historical series at www.ggdc.net, accessed July 2012

Figure 10.1 Two millennia of population and production

It is important to see that real GPP grows for two reasons. Firstly, population grows so that total production increases because the number of workers increases. Secondly, workers become more productive as knowledge builds and more capital goods become available: their productivity increases (that is the units of output in relation to the units of input). Figure 10.2 summarizes twenty centuries of real average annual GPP growth and its drivers, presenting a statistical decomposition by means of the growth rate of the population and productivity, respectively. You can see that the 2000s are exceptional because in this period the rate of population growth decreases, while productivity increases (but note that the data unfortunately stop in 2008 and thus do not cover the impact of the financial and economic crisis).

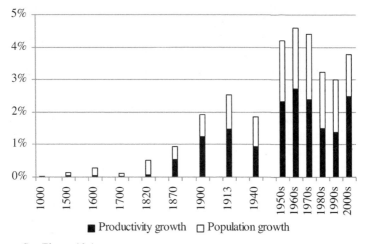

Source: See Figure 10.1

Figure 10.2   Two millennia of the drivers of real GPP growth (end of period, annual averages)

Figure 10.3 shows the same decomposition for GPP growth for the years 1951 – 2008 because for this period annual data are available. It is evident from the figure that population growth has been a stable force since the Second World War: on average the growth rate was 1.7 per cent with a standard deviation of 0.3. Because of this stability we will most of the time treat the growth rate of Earth's population (and of its labour force) as an exogenously determined factor. Figure 10.3 also illustrates that productivity increases have on the whole contributed more to real post Second World War economic growth as the average annual increase is 2.25 per cent. Earth's productivity has fluctuated more strongly than population (the standard deviation was 1.3). Actually, and in contrast to population in the post Second World War period, negative numbers do sometimes occur for Earth's productivity growth, for example in the aftermath of the first and second oil shocks (1975, 1982) and in 1991 as a consequence of the oil price spike during the Gulf War. Also note that GPP growth (that is the total of productivity growth and population growth) never turns negative.

A low level of productivity growth is also evident in 1998 when the Asian crisis hit the world economy. It is interesting to see if and how we can explain these findings.

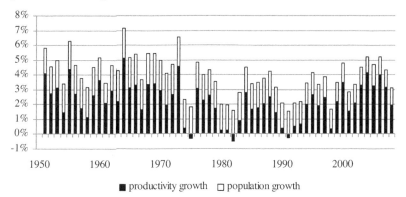

Source: See Figure 10.1

Figure 10.3 Drivers of real GPP growth (1951 – 2008, end of period, annual averages)

Exercise 10.1 Growth in the 1980s to 2000s
- Compare Figures 3.5 and 10.3 and see where real GPP growth data agree and differ.
- Try to explain the differences.

10.1 EARTH'S PRODUCTION, THE CAPITAL STOCK AND THE DYNAMICS OF GROWTH

How do we produce? Of course someone will have to do the actual work, that is: he or she must use part of his or her time in the production process. This amount of time is the labour input L. Most of the time workers will use equipment (or more generally capital). This can range from a hammer to a personal computer and from an engine to a plough. The total capital stock that is used in the production process is denoted by K. We can write the production function that states that production Q results from combining K and L, as $Q=Q(K,L)$. (Note that we will write labour productivity q as Q/L)

The production function and its actual form are at the heart of the economic analysis of long term growth. We already had a discussion of the production function in Section 8.3. This chapter is different because we no longer take the capital stock as given.

Of course the capital stock is not like manna from heaven. K itself by necessity has been produced in the past. These capital goods are the goods that were produced, but not consumed and thus we can see the capital stock as the sum of all past investments I taking depreciation D into account. This method is called the perpetual inventory method. Basically, the method states $K_t = \Sigma I_n - D_n$ where n refers to all previous years. This method obviously requires a lot of data and often we will therefore simply assume that depreciation is a fixed percentage d (the rate of depreciation) so that $K_t = \Sigma(1 - d)I_n$. If we consider the capital stock's change ΔK we get $\Delta K = (1 - d) I$.

The Harrod-Domar Model

Now let's for the moment consider a simple production function with fixed technical coefficients (as illustrated in the left-hand side of Diagrams 8.7 and 8.8). Such a production function assumes that you cannot substitute labour and capital. This is a reasonable assumption in the short term: running a machine requires a given number of workers and it will not help much if you increase the number of idle hands. On the other hand you cannot expect that a machine will run properly if there are insufficient workers. So in order to produce 1 unit of output you will need at least κ machines (units of K) and α units of labour L (and to produce 2 units you need at least 2κ and 2α and so on). Typically one of these factors is the bottleneck and that determines how much you are going to produce. For example, if both κ and α are ½ and we have $L = 5$ and $K = 4$, then K is the bottleneck and output equals $K/\kappa = 8$. We can write this formally as:

$$Q = \min\left[\frac{K}{\kappa}, \frac{L}{\alpha}\right] \tag{10.1}$$

This equation is an example of the Harrod-Domar production function. In many discussions K is considered to be the bottleneck and labour is assumed to be available in sufficient quantities. Under this assumption (see, however, Text Box 10.1) we can write the production function as $Q = K/\kappa$. The next step is to describe the process of building the capital stock and here we can borrow from Part I that saving equals investment so we have

$$\Delta K = (1 - d) I = S = sQ. \tag{10.2}$$

Text Box 10.1   Labour can become a bottleneck: world population pyramids 1950 – 2050

You may want to doubt the assumption that labour is not a bottleneck given the fact that the world population is ageing and that this will reduce labour participation (Figure 10.4; working age shares are in black). Whereas in the 1950s less than 6 per cent of the world population was 65 years and older, by 2050 almost 1 out of 5 humans will be old-aged. Another factor that may make certain types of labour already scarce in the current context is that in addition to the quantity also the quality of labour is very important. This implies that it is important to consider the level of education as well. If anything it is dangerous to extend this assumption far into the future.

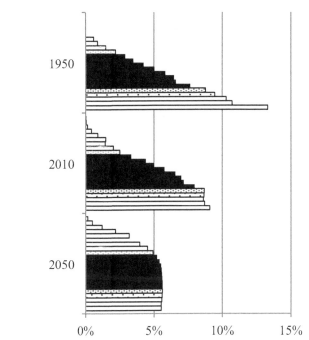

Source: UN population prospects data base esa.un.org/unpd/wpp June 2012

Figure 10.4 Population pyramids 1950 – 2050 (per cent of age cohort)

So each period the economy saves and invests sQ thus raising the capital stock K. Next we can take first differences: $\Delta Q = {}^{1}\!/s\Delta I$ (which is nothing more than the multiplier process introduced in Chapter 2; you will remember that $s = 1 - c$) and we also have $\Delta Q = {}^1/\kappa\, \Delta K = {}^1/\kappa\, (1 - d)\, I$. We can now combine the two expressions for ΔQ, so: ${}^1/s\Delta I = {}^1/\kappa\, (1 - d)$ in order to arrive at

$$\frac{\Delta I}{I} = \frac{s(1-d)}{\kappa} \qquad\qquad (10.3)$$

so that the rate of investment growth is given by $s(1 - d)/\kappa$ the ratio of the net savings rate s_n to the capital-output ratio $\kappa = K/Q$ with $s_n = (1 - d)s$. Since I and Q have a fixed ratio of s, we know that the rate of growth of production must also equal s_n/κ. At this rate the expectations of investors are being fulfilled and capital will be fully employed. Stronger growth is technically not possible and lower growth will leave capital idle and is not efficient (actually if capital is not used this will act as a disincentive for investment). The growth rate, however, can be increased if κ decreases (so if capital productivity increases, for example because new technologies are introduced) or if the saving rate is increased.

Application at the World Level

Let us for the purpose of illustration try to put some numbers on this equation. We have seen earlier (Figure 4.1) that gross savings is averaging around 22 per cent of Earth's GPP. Assuming a depreciation rate of 0.1 (thus that 10% of capital needs to be depreciated each year) we find that the net saving rate $s_n = (1 - d)s = (1 - 0.1)\, 0.22 = 0.9 \cdot 0.22$ or about 0.2.

Regarding the capital-output ratio we have the recent ballpark figure that was produced by the World Bank (2011b) report *The Changing Wealth of Nations: Measuring Sustainable Development in the New Millennium*. This report provides detailed estimates at the national level of natural capital, produced capital and 'intangible capital' (Figure 10.5). The latter category includes institutions, knowledge and social capital. All these factors are important and relevant of course, but the output would be wealth rather than production. Since we are interested in GPP we have to limit ourselves to the more traditional forms of capital, that is: natural capital (exhaustible resources, renewable resources and agricultural land) and produced capital (buildings, machinery, equipment and infrastructure).

Figure 10.5 provides us with two estimates of κ, namely for the ratio of produced capital to GPP of 2.7 and the ratio of (produced and natural capital) to GPP of 3.4.

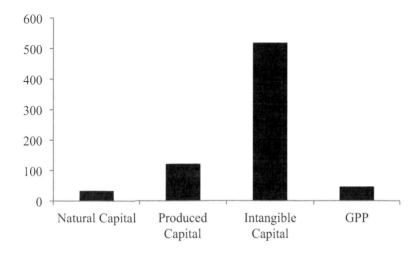

Sources: World Bank (2011b, p.7) and IMF WEO April 2012 database

Figure 10.5 Earth capital stock 2005 (trillions of US$)

Taking these estimates into account (so for $2.7 < \kappa < 3.4$) we find that the warranted rate of growth of investment equals 5.8 to 7.3 which is a bit in excess of the rate of real GPP growth that we observed Figure 10.3 for the 2000s. The implication is that the warranted growth rate exceeds the natural rate (defined as the sum of population growth and productivity growth) so that according to the model excess capacity develops.

Exercise 10.2 Harrod-Domar model
- Analyse the growth impact of an increase in saving.
- Compare your result with the Keynesian model of Chapter 5.

The Harrod-Domar model has been quite influential in the early phase of empirical development economics. The model was used to estimate savings and trade gaps for individual countries and the required amounts of development aid (see Chenery and Strout 1966; this option of external resource flows obviously does not exist for the planet as a whole). You will often find this kind of production function in the older literature using for example the basic expression that $\Delta Q = {}^{1}/\kappa\,(1-d)\,I$, basically because the data requirements for this simple approach are limited and can also be met when statistical offices are not yet at a more advanced level. Recently the model has been used by the UN, the World Bank and the OECD to estimate the costs of reaching the Millennium Development Goals (see Atisophon et al. 2011, that also discusses earlier results).

10.2   THE NEOCLASSICAL GROWTH MODEL

Once we relax the assumption of fixed technical coefficients, we can allow for substitution between the factors of production. This means that we assume that firms can increase their production by, for example, increasing the amount of capital while leaving the amount of labour used in the production process at a constant level. Obviously substitution takes time and thus this assumption deals with the longer term. The production function is quite general and can be written as $Q = F(K, L)$ and we only require that the marginal product F_K and F_L are both positive and decreasing as K and L increase, respectively. So the second derivatives F_{KK} and F_{LL} are both negative. This implies that production grows when we add one unit of a production factor, but that the contribution of an additional unit is smaller (this is the law of diminishing returns). It is further useful to assume constant returns to scale, that is: the function F is homogeneous of degree one in both production factors so we have $\lambda Q = F(\lambda K, \lambda L)$ or in words: if we increase both inputs by the same percentage, then the output will also increase by that percentage. This is a useful property since we can now set $\lambda = {}^1/L$ so that we get $q = Q/L = F({}^K/_L, 1)$ or $q = f(k)$ where k is the capital-labour ratio ${}^K/_L$ and $f_k > 0$ and we require $f_{kk} < 0$.

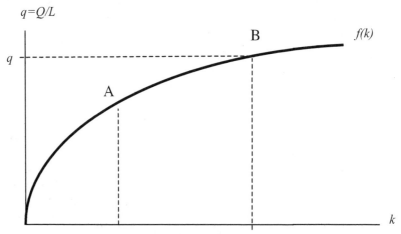

Diagram 10.1 Solow production function in per capita terms

Diagram 10.1 presents the production function. An increase in k gives a movement on the curve. The relationship between labour productivity q and the capital-labour ratio k is an important stepping stone for understanding what factors drive long term growth. An increase in the capital stock per worker k increases his productivity q as is illustrated in Diagram 10.1 by the movement from point A to point B on the production function f. Productivity increases through the process of capital deepening that occurs when the amount of capital per worker increases.

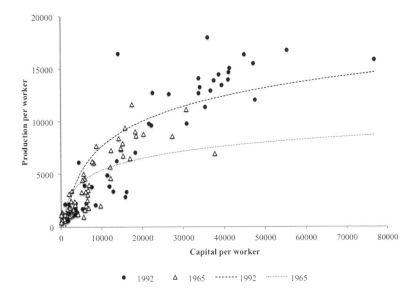

Source: Heston et al. (2002)

Figure 10.6 World labour productivity and capital per worker in 1965 and 1992 (at international 1985 prices and dollars)

Figure 10.6 depicts the capital to worker ratio and the production per worker ratio for a large number of countries in 1965 and 1992 (the most recent year for which comprehensive estimates for capital per worker are available). Added to the observations are dotted (dashed) regression lines for 1965 (1992). Note that these lines are summary measures for the data and should not be interpreted as production functions. With this caveat in mind, Figure 10.6 shows capital deepening (the amount of capital per worker roughly doubles in a quarter of a century) and higher productivity per unit of capital (an increase by about half over the same period).

Exercise 10.3 Solow production function
- What factors shift the production function in Diagram 10.1 upward?

Note, however, that if the economy is and remains in point B (so that $\Delta q = 0$), the economy's production Q still grows with the rate of growth of the labour force. Eartheconomic production in a situation represented by point B is thus not stationary.

Now we can write down the neoclassical growth model for the Earth economy:

Equilibrium condition:	$I = S$	(10.4)
Saving function:	$S = sQ$	(10.5)
Capital accumulation:	$\Delta K = I - dK$	(10.6)
Definition equation capital-labour ratio:	$k = {}^K/_L$	(10.7)
Definition equation labour productivity:	$q = {}^Q/_L$	(10.8)
Behavioural: labour grows exogenously:	${}^{\Delta L}/_L = n$	(10.9)

Endogenous: $I, S, Q, \Delta K, K, k, q,$ and L
Exogenous: $s, d,$ and n

Obviously, we have fewer equations than endogenous variables, so we cannot solve for the equilibrium value of k, but we can say something about the underlying process. Substitute (10.4) and (10.5) in (10.6) and divide by L in order to get ${}^{\Delta K}/_L = sq - dk$. We also have from (10.7) that ${}^{\Delta k}/_k \approx {}^{\Delta K}/_K - {}^{\Delta L}/_L$ which we rewrite as $\Delta K = K({}^{\Delta k}/_k - {}^{\Delta L}/_L)$. Substitute (10.9) and divide by L and now we have ${}^{\Delta K}/_L = k({}^{\Delta k}/_k - n) = \Delta k - nk$. Next we use both expressions for ${}^{\Delta K}/_L$ in order to get $sq - dk = k({}^{\Delta k}/_k - n)$ which we rewrite as the fundamental equation of capital accumulation:

$$\Delta k = sq - (n+d)k. \qquad (10.10)$$

The fundamental equation of capital accumulation is very useful and helps us to understand basic properties of productivity growth. We can, for example, use the fundamental equation to illustrate that saving is necessary to simply keep the amount of capital per worker constant. Keeping the capital-labour ratio constant implies $\Delta k = 0$. So using (10.10) we have $sq = (n+d)k$. That is to say that the savings per worker sq must equal capital per worker k times the sum of the growth of the labour force n and the depreciation rate d. If the economy meets these requirements the increase in the capital stock exactly accommodates the increase of the labour force at a constant level of capital per worker. This is a situation of capital widening in which K grows just quickly enough to keep the capital-labour ratio constant when the labour force grows: more workers get capital but unlike the situation of capital deepening the average amount of capital per worker remains constant. Capital deepening occurs when the capital-labour ratio increases (so that we have $\Delta k > 0$) which requires $sq > (n+d)k$.

The neoclassical growth model is illustrated in Diagram 10.2. We introduce the savings function sq and use a ray through the origin to represent the condition $(n+d)k$. In point A we have the equality $sq = (n+d)k$, the capital labour ratio is k_A, the level of labour productivity is q_A and the level of saving per worker is sq_A. In a point to the left of A we would have that sq exceeds $(n+d)k$ so there $\Delta k > 0$ and we would see capital deepening increasing the capital-labour ratio leading to a movement along the production function towards point A. The opposite happens in points to the right of A, so A is a stable equilibrium.

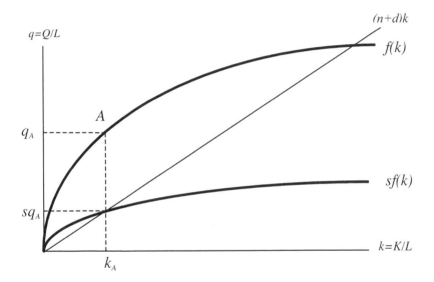

Diagram 10.2 The neoclassical growth model

Exercise 10.4 Solow model
- Determine the average consumption rate at point A (Diagram 10.2).
- Analyse the impact of an increase in the consumption rate.
- Compare your result with the Keynesian model of Chapter 5.

Note that the fact, that A is an equilibrium, does not mean that this is a good situation. Actually the economy would be much better off at a $k > k_A$, but the model shows that simply increasing the amount of capital per worker would be inconsistent with the underlying conditions and that the economy would be driven back to the equilibrium level. For higher productivity we need capital deepening and this can be achieved in three ways: lower growth of the workforce and lower depreciation (so taking better care of equipment) which reduces the slope of the $(n+d)k$ ray and higher saving which shifts the saving function upward.

Now let us assume that the saving rate increases at time $t = 0$. How does the growth adjustment process work? Diagram 10.3 shows the upward shift of the saving function ($s_1 > s_0$). Note that this is the only shift that occurs in the diagram. The condition $(n+d)k$ is not influenced by the change in saving behaviour and neither is the production function. So what we observe is that the equilibrium moves along the production function from point A to point B where it arrives at $t = 1$, say. This movement represents an endogenous increase from q_A to q_B caused by the capital-labour ratio move from k_A to k_B.

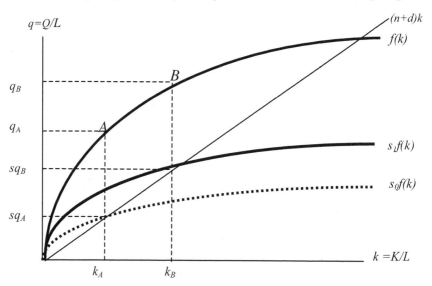

Diagram 10.3 Increase in savings rate

Diagram 10.4 shows how this increase in the saving rate translates into time paths for productivity, productivity growth and production growth. The top panel of Diagram 10.4 reflects the increase in the productivity level that we derived in Diagram 10.3. The middle panel translates this into the rate of growth of productivity. Before $t = 0$ productivity is stable, it grows between $t = 0$ and $t = 1$ and is stable again after this transition period. The rate of growth of production is positive all the time because it always includes the rate of growth of the labour force n. During the transition period the rate of growth is temporarily higher, but in the end the economy grows again at a constant rate although the level of production is always higher than on the previous growth path.

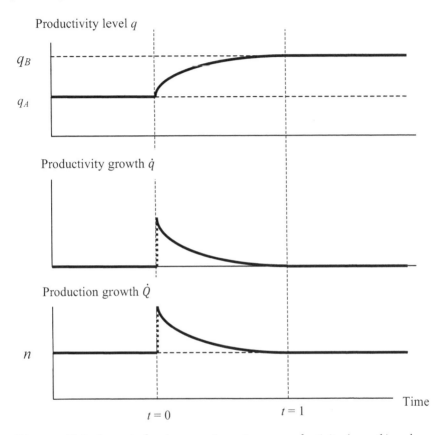

Diagram 10.4 Impact of an increase in saving on productivity (growth) and production growth

Diagram 10.5 shows how this pattern influences the pattern of growth of production Q. The left-hand panel shows the level of production and the right hand panel shows the logarithm of that level. Taking logs helps you to see directly the growth rate as this is now the inclination of the function.

Exercise 10.5 Rate of growth
*   Compare in Diagram 10.5 the rate of growth before, during and after the transitory phase.

Q Log Q

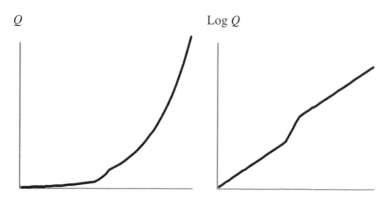

Diagram 10.5 Transitory growth trajectories

10.3   GROWTH ACCOUNTING

The Solow model helps us to theoretically understand the underlying processes and drivers of economic growth. This is useful of course, but if we want to investigate the sources of economic growth empirically we would like to do that from a more open and less framed perspective, for example because we recognize that conditions of time and place determine the appropriateness of theoretical concepts. Growth accounting is a technique that does not presuppose such a theoretical structure and allows us to find out the contributions of each of the factors of production to economic growth.

The starting point is a production function $Q = Q(K, L, T)$ that describes how capital K, labour L and technology T are combined to produce output Q. We keep this function as general as possible and do not enforce any restrictions on the curvature. We take the first derivative of the production function and get

$$dQ = Q_K dK + Q_L dL + Q_T dT \qquad (10.11)$$

Here Q_K is the marginal product of capital or R/P (the real return on capital) and Q_L is the marginal product of labour or W/P (real wage). Divide (10.11) by Q and rewrite

$$dQ/Q = R/PQ \, dK + W/PQ \, dL + Q_T/Q dT \qquad (10.12)$$

Multiply (10.12) by K/K and L/L and write growth rates as g_Q, g_K and g_L in order to get:

$$g_Q = RK/PQ \; g_K + WL/PQ \; g_L + Q_T/Q \; dT$$

g_Q=capital share $\bullet$ g_K + labour share $\bullet$ g_L + Solow residual

So the growth rate of production is decomposed into the growth contribution of capital (the capital share multiplied by the growth rate of the capital stock) and the growth contribution of labour (the labour share multiplied by the growth rate of the employed labour force) and a component that is called the 'Solow residual'. It is named after Solow who in 1957 developed the growth accounting framework. It is clear, however, that the Solow residual actually measures the impact of all other factors (that is of anything used in addition to capital and labour). It is often referred to as 'manna from heaven' and a 'measure of ignorance' because it blends the impact of changes in aggregate efficiency (due to, for example, structural reforms or more vigorous competition policy) and the impact of omitted variables (such as land, energy and education). A more complimentary label for the Solow residual is Total Factor Productivity (TFP) that can be defined as the part of economic growth that is not explained by changes in capital and labour. Typically the 'residual' explains a substantial part of growth.

Exercise 10.6 Solow residual
- Derive the labour share in the manufacturing sector from Table 2.3.
- Typically economic researchers set the labour share at 2/3; why would this be different from your answer on the previous question?

Application to World Data 1965 – 1992

Using the data set that was used to construct Figure 10.6 we can summarize the approximate annual growth rates of output and the factors of production for an aggregate of 50 countries for which the data are available both in 1965 and 1992 (so this is not global data and excludes for example China, India, Brazil and Russia). Aggregates are expressed in constant 1985 prices. For this aggregate output Q grows at 3.3% *p.a.*, the capital stock K grows at 4.7% *p.a.* and the population L at 1.6% *p.a.* We assume a labour share of 70% and a capital share of 30%. Thus the portion of growth in output which is due to changes in factors is 0.7 $\bullet$ 1.6 + 0.3 $\bullet$ 4.7 = 2.5. Total Factor Productivity (the Solow residual) is 3.3 − 2.5 = 0.8 which is almost a quarter of Earth's observed output growth and about a third of the output growth that can be explained by the growth of capital and labour.

Exercise 10.7 Growth accounting 1995-2005

The world's capital stock at constant 2005 prices increases from $91 trillion in 1995 to $121 trillion in 2005. Over the same period global employment increases from 2.41 to 2.85 billion persons. Real GPP grows at 3.8% *p.a.* Assume a labour share of 70% and a capital share of 30%.

- Calculate TFP and compare your result with the period 1965-1992.

10.4   KEY CONCEPTS

- Bottle neck
- Capital deepening
- Capital stock
- Capital widening
- Capital-labour ratio
- Fixed technical coefficients
- Fundamental equation of capital accumulation
- Growth accounting
- Harrod-Domar model
- Intangible capital

- Law of diminishing returns
- Natural capital
- Net saving rate
- Produceable capital
- Productivity
- Solow model
- Solow residual
- Substitution
- Total factor productivity (TFP)

11. Development and Change

This chapter deals with one of the most challenging eartheconomic issues, namely development. I will take an economic approach to this issue and define development as an increase in *per capita* income that is sustainable in view of the concomitant improvement of productivity levels (but note that Chapter 12 takes up the issue of environmental sustainability and limits to growth). It should of course be acknowledged that development defined in this manner is narrow and neglects important dimensions of equity, opportunity and genetic inheritance and predestination. The Dutch Nobel Prize laureate in Economics, Jan Tinbergen, often pointed out that the two most grave injustices in the world are, firstly, the place where your crib was erected and, secondly, the IQ that you received. There is much wisdom in Tinbergen's observation, but considering these issues introduces the need to consider value judgements.

I appreciate the wisdom of this statement in full, but in this chapter it is economics and not morality that determines what we will discuss. Without global growth it will be much more difficult to achieve a fair(er) division of income and opportunities. This is why we focus on economic growth in the present chapter and deal with issues of efficiency rather than equity. Basically we will study how structural reforms and other policies could ignite or re-start global growth. This is a somewhat controversial topic given the fact that structural reforms aimed at larger openness, stiffer competition, and smaller government (that means: privatization) form part of the so-called Washington Consensus that is now contested by many.

The plan of the chapter is simple. We will use Solow's neoclassical model to investigate how humanity can theoretically get the growth process going. This problem can only be solved if we first take a close look at crucial factors and settings that actually prohibit the emergence of steady and sustained real *per capita* growth. Therefore we will first of all be interested in the so-called poverty (or growth) traps that explain why growth processes do not take off and relatedly offer potential escape routes from poverty. Next we will look at the potential for structural reform to help the growth agenda.

11.1   POVERTY TRAP IN THE SOLOW MODEL

Diagram 11.1 shows how a poverty trap could emerge in the standard Solow model. The model shown is a lookalike of Diagrams 10.1 and 10.2, but with one crucial difference and that is the curvature of the production function (and thus of the saving function) that although still monotonously increasing now has sections where productivity increases steeply (the curve eventually may flatten out at higher levels of q and k).

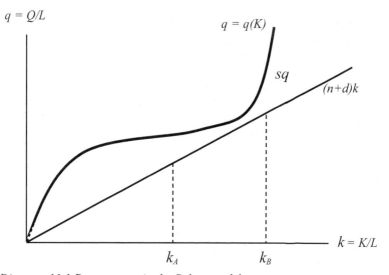

Diagram 11.1 Poverty trap in the Solow model

The $(n+d)k$ ray and the savings function have two intersections now (and the equilibrium capital-labour ratios are marked k_A and k_B in Diagram 11.1) So rather than one equilibrium we have now two equilibria in the Solow model: one at a relatively low level (k_A) and one at a relatively high level (k_B).

Exercise 11.1 Poverty trap
- Check the stability of k_A and k_B in Diagram 11.1.
- Explain the adjustment process toward k_A (taking both lower and higher capital-labour ratios as your point of departure).

In Diagram 11.1, the economy will develop towards the level $q(k_A)$; that is: until the capital-labour ratio reaches the level of k_A. Between k_A and k_B the economy will fall back to the level of $q(k_A)$. An intuitive interpretation is that a certain level of capital goods (for example essential infrastructure including roads, harbours, communication, etc.) is necessary before the economy can really take off. This level k_B thus acts as an hurdle. Until the economy passes the hurdle it will always fall back to the low development level q_A. This part of the model looks a lot like the vice and misery that some of the classical political economists (such as Malthus and Ricardo) in the eighteenth century sketched as the grim future for the human species. However, the Solow model is more optimistic because once the economy passes the k_B hurdle it will start on a sustained growth path. This path mimics the growth paths suggested by the early endogenous growth theories. These theories essentially argue against decreasing marginal productivity for reproducible production factors including knowledge (education, research and development) and capital. If marginal productivity is not decreasing productivity can grow forever.

One important policy question is of course: can the world indeed escape from the low development trap? If you take a look at Figures 10.1 and 10.2 you know the answer: 'Yes we can!' The next section studies how the Solow model can help us to understand how this can be achieved.

11.2 ESCAPE ROUTES: SAVING, FERTILITY, INNOVATION AND EFFICIENCY

The Solow model offers four recipes to escape from the poverty trap: increase saving per capita, reduce population growth, innovate, and enhance efficiency. These four strategies are of course not mutually exclusive. Indeed, the probability of escaping from a poverty trap increases if the strategies are combined. Note that the Solow model provides a very stylized representation of economic development. The model does not give a road map for development. It shows which economic factors are important but many other impediments to growth may be responsible for keeping an economy at a low-income-low-productivity equilibrium, such as institutional factors or insufficient public infrastructure. With this caveat in mind let us study how an economy can escape from the poverty trap in the Solow model.

Increase Saving

The first escape route is illustrated in Diagram 11.2. The royal road to economic growth is an increase in the saving rate. This is a matter of sacrificing consumption for a limited period of time.

Indeed, once the economy passes the hurdle rate k_B saving rates can be relaxed again, because the economy has now been launched onto a self-sustaining growth path.

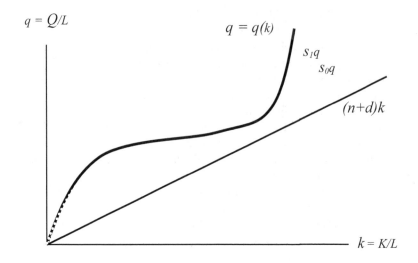

$q = Q/L$

$q = q(k)$

$s_1 q$

$s_0 q$

$(n+d)k$

$k = K/L$

Diagram 11.2   Increase in saving rate provides an escape from the poverty trap

---

Exercise 11.2 Higher saving provides an escape from the poverty trap
- Explain why saving only needs to be higher for a relatively short period of time.

One important implication of this model is that saving may actually be necessary to get an economy growing again. This is a lesson that is often forgotten by policy makers that argue that consumers should spend more to grow out of a crisis. At the global level more spending means less saving and thus less capital accumulation, reducing future growth potential.

Reduce Population Growth

Diagram 11.3 shows a second escape route: reduce population growth (again: at least for some time until the take off launches you above the critical level). Reducing the population growth rate from n_0 to n_1 shifts the $(n+d)k$ ray down so that capital deepening is stimulated and productivity growth sets in. The Chinese one-child policy might be viewed as an extreme example of this manner of policy. It would, however, also seem that development, education and anti-conception worked at the global level: in 1950 about 44 per cent of the world population had a total fertility of 6 or more children. By 2010, the population with a total fertility of more than 6 children according to the UN (2011) declined to less than 2 per cent. Figure 11.1 reports the development of world fertility numbers for 1950 – 2050.

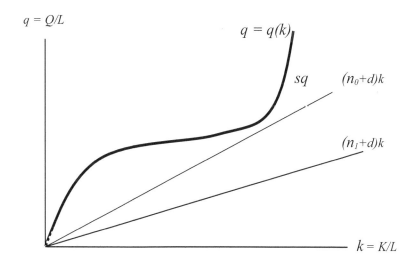

Diagram 11.3 Lower population growth can get the economy out of the poverty trap

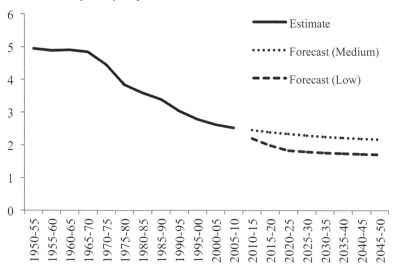

Source: UN population prospects data base esa.un.org/unpd/wpp June 2012

Figure 11.1 World fertility (children per woman) 1950 – 2050

Innovate

Innovation brings new and better products and enables old products to be used in new combinations. Innovation can be very powerful as illustrated in Figure 11.2 that shows how the number of mobile phones has developed. In less than half a generation the old system of landlines and fixed telephones has been transformed into a global system of interconnected consumers that can have access to global communication networks.

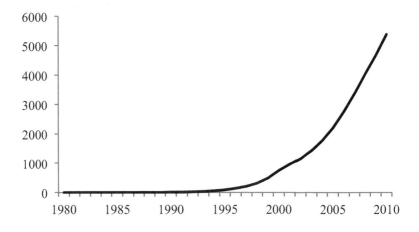

Source: World DataBank (accessed: July 2012)

Figure 11.2 World mobile cellular subscriptions (millions, 1980 – 2010)

Technology shifts the production function (and the saving function in its slipstream) upward. In Diagram 11.4 you will note a shift from q_0 to q_1 and therefore also a shift of the saving function from sq_0 to sq_1. With the ray $(n + d)k$ remaining unchanged at its original location, you will observe that sq_1 does no longer intersect with $(n + d)k$ so that the economy passes the hurdle level k_B and is launched on an upward growth trajectory.

Enhance Efficiency

Increasing efficiency means that more can be produced with the same inputs. Hence at all levels of the capital-labour ratio the productivity will increase: enhanced efficiency shifts the production function and the saving function upward. Diagram 11.4 thus portrays the impact both of more innovation and of more efficiency.

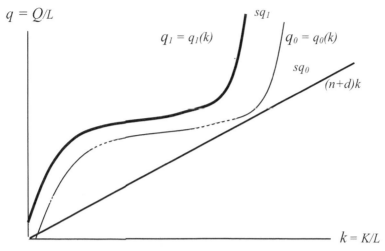

Diagram 11.4 Innovation and efficiency enhancement shift the production function up and lift the economy out of the poverty trap

---

Exercise 11.3 Depreciation and the poverty trap
- Could depreciation offer an escape from the poverty trap?

Although we have labelled the growth trap above as a poverty trap, it should be noted that the problems and solutions are not only relevant for the poorest countries. Lin and Rosenblatt (2012, p. 8), for example, identify a middle income growth trap. Escaping from the middle income trap may require enhanced efficiency, for example, by means of structural reforms that shift the production function upwards.

11.3 A CLOSER LOOK AT STRUCTURAL REFORM

Structural reform is often seen as an instrument to enhance the efficiency of the economy. Privatization, deregulation, reregulation, liberalization etc. are assumed to stimulate competition and that in its turn enhances efficiency. This is the mantra of the OECD's structural reform agenda and of the Washington Consensus, that both have been very influential in framing and shaping structural reform policies around the globe. Figure 11.3 by way of illustration reports the jurisdictions with and without a competition law in 1980 and 2005 testifying to the tsunami of competition legislation in the 1980s and 1990s.

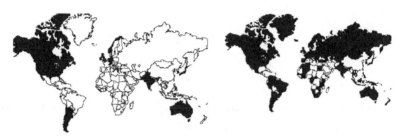

Source: ICN (2005)

Figure 11.3 Countries with a competition law in 1980 (left) and 2005 (right)

Structural reform does, however, not always and unambiguously have a positive impact on key economic variables. This may be very basic. The Exchequer may prefer monopolies because they are highly profitable and thus add substantially to tax revenues. The Central Banker is the friend of the monopolist because competitive economies will adjust prices fully to cost shocks (and competition may also threaten the soundness of banking). Trade unions probably appreciate the higher wages that are paid by firms with market power.

Diagram 11.5 illustrates yet another – and often overlooked – consequence of structural reform, namely the ambiguous impact on the labour market. The top panel of Diagram 11.5 shows eartheconomic demand and supply. The economy is at Q_0 below the full employment equilibrium Q_1, because distortions in the economy have created a wedge between demand and supply. An example could be an economy with a lax competition law and/or competition authority. This generates a mark-up of prices over costs.

Exercise 11.4 Mark-up
- Identify the mark-up of the market distortion in Diagram 11.5.

Now let us investigate what happens if more vigorous competition policies are applied worldwide. Undoubtedly this is beneficial for the economy that moves from Q_0 to Q_1 and at the same time the general price level decreases as market prices move towards competitive levels.

The bottom panel of Diagram 11.5 shows what happens with labour demand. The panel looks new but actually it is the production function that has been flipped so that we have input (labour L) on the vertical axis and output (production Q) on the horizontal axis. Now it is clear that production is moving towards the full employment equilibrium and normally that would of course increase demand for labour.

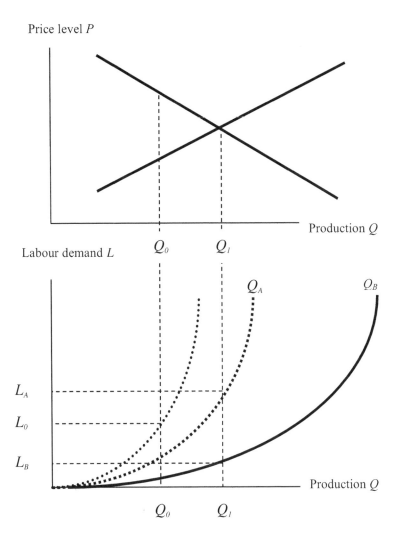

*Diagram 11.5 Impact of structural reform on the product and the labour
        market*

However, due to the structural reform measures firms become more
efficient so that labour productivity increases. We have now two options: the
increase in eartheconomic demand is stronger than the increase in labour
productivity so that labour demand increases to L_A or the increase in labour
productivity exceeds the increase in eartheconomic demand so that labour
demand actually falls to L_B. The implication is that a policy of structural

reforms can ignite growth, but that its impact on employment and unemployment is uncertain. The stronger the increase in productivity the lower the probability that jobs will be created.

Exercise 11.5 Structural reform
- Can the economy in Diagram 11.5 reach the full employment level without structural reform?
- Analyse the impact of structural reform on the wage rate using Diagram 11.5.

11.4   KEY CONCEPTS

- Competition
- Development
- Efficiency
- Endogenous growth
- Fertility
- Innovation

- Middle income trap
- Population growth
- Poverty trap
- Structural reform
- Washington Consensus

12. Limits to Growth?

Some see the short-term fluctuations that we studied in the previous Part, in particular in Chapter 3, as the ripples on the larger waves that they perceive to be governing economic conditions. The long waves both have a lower frequency (so that it takes longer to move from peak to trough and back again) and an amplitude that is sufficiently large to influence long term averages (whereas the peaks and troughs of the short-term business cycles are assumed to average out). Another way to say this is that during the rise of the wave we see more periods of prosperity than during the downturn. These larger waves, which thus take much more time both to build and to be recognized, are the topic of the present chapter. Whereas the short-term fluctuations often dominate the newspapers and the policy debate, the long movements play the main role in history books and often can be recognized in characterizations of periods such as the Golden Decade of Keynesianism for the 1950s and 1960s. In such periods policies and the economy reinforce each other and may thus yield either very good or very bad results. It should be noted that long wave theories typically become popular in economic downturns (probably because it holds the promise of an unavoidable upturn) so it is expected that long waves will return to the top of the research agenda again. An important element of the long wave is that it suggests that there are endogenous limits to high growth eras (and that is a lesson that is often forgotten in the optimistic decade(s) preceding a global downturn).

Long waves have already been documented for the 14th Century B.C.: 'Behold, there come seven years of great plenty throughout all the land of Egypt: and there shall arise after them seven years of famine' (Genesis 41: 29). It should, however, be noted that the earliest statistical observations of long waves in modern economics date back to only the 1930s and the evidence for the existence of the cycles is still to be considered preliminary and highly contested, also because dating the longest wave (which since the Industrial Revolution at most has passed through five full cycles) is problematic.

Table 12.1 summarizes the categories of long economic waves that have so far been recognized (typically the waves are named after their 'inventors'), based on Schumpeter (1954). The four different waves are nowadays typically identified with investment processes. During an upswing investment increases generate the overcapacity that eventually leads to a downturn. The excess capacity is especially caused by the fact that firms have difficulty in observing when the cycle turns and also need time to make decisions and adjust. The duration of the cycle reflects the time needed to produce the capital goods. The Kitchin wave is derived from inventories (remember that inventories are part of investment). The Juglar wave reflects fixed investments in machinery and buildings, so an adaption of long-run full employment supply levels. The Kuznets wave is seen as a consequence of investments in infrastructure, by far the most time consuming kind of investment. Finally the Kondratieff wave has been linked to discoveries of new products and clusters of innovations that provide leading technologies and stimulate the take off phase of the wave.

Table 12.1 Economic waves

Wave	Driver(s)	Duration in years
Kitchin	Inventories	3 to5
Juglar	Fixed investment	7 to 11
Kuznets	Infrastructure	15 to 25
Kondratieff	War, Mass moods, Innovation, Credit cycle Debt, Demography	40 to 60

12.1 THE KONDRATIEFF WAVE

In the 1930s the long cycles were observed mainly in price data and therefore theoretical explanations at that time predominantly considered monetary explanations. Kondratieff, who is credited for discovering the longest cycle, was convinced that the drivers and the impact of the cycle were much more broadly based in social sciences and psychology: '... the long waves, if existent at all, are a very important and essential factor in economic development, a factor the effects of which can be found in all the principal fields of social and economic life' (Kondratieff 1935, p. 115).

Kondratieff was able to detect only three waves of about 50 years, because the available statistics did not cover a longer period, but he saw remarkable similarities during the downturns and upturns of the cycle, for example that wars were by and large located in the upswing, that new markets were opened during the upswing and that important discoveries occurred during recession but were only applied and commercialized during the upturn. Nowadays five cycles of the Kondratieff wave are recognized that have been defined by lead technologies and production methods (*i*) the industrial revolution; (*ii*) steel, steam and railways; (*iii*) electrical engineering; (*iv*) automobiles and petrochemicals; (*v*) information and telecommunications.

Diagram 12.1 provides a modern day representation of the characteristics and drivers of the long wave. Typically four phases are distinguished. The upturn (Summer) is the phase in which prices increase. After the turning point economic growth and inflation slow down during the Autumn of the long wave. In the Winter growth and inflation can become negative leading to depression and deflation. The upturn in the Spring of the long wave brings growth and modest inflation.

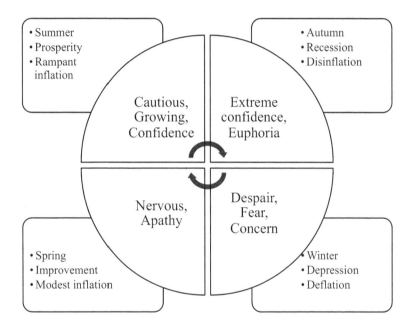

Diagram 12.1 Summer, autumn, winter and spring characteristics of the Kondratieff wave

The interesting proposition is that the economic characteristics feed into the general psychological climate and in their turn the economic developments are of course also influenced by those mass moods (see also the earlier discussion on the Keynesian theory about Animal Spirits in Chapter 5).

Collective Memory and the Creation of Knowledge

The length of the long wave suggests that the depreciation of human capital may play a role, in particular in the case of Black Swans. A Black Swan is a large-impact, low-probability event (Taleb 2007). Large impact events are engraved in our collective memory and form part of formal and informal education by the older generations. If the frequency of the event is sufficiently high collective knowledge will be built and transferred between generations. This is even true for low-frequency events. My students, for example, are able to tell me about crises that occurred long before they were born because they had to endure the stories of their parents. They will do the same with their children, but the point is that their stories will be different because their lifetime Black Swans will be different (Papenhausen 2008).

Low-probability high-impact events therefore tend to be forgotten, neglected and ignored. This is a general phenomenon. The process of learning is heuristic and iterative: typically such processes can be described as empirical cycles of observation, analysis, proposal, implementation or testing and evaluation. The process of scientific discovery and the practise of policy development provide examples. Typically, the development of theory and policy during low-frequency high-economic-impact events such as a global depression is characterized by uncertainty of developments and outcomes and by constant learning about the actual real world conditions. Hypotheses are formulated about possible 'states of the world'. As more evidence/information becomes available the probabilities of the different possible states of the world are re-evaluated: the weight of evidence determines perceived probabilities of alternative explanations. Now it is important to realise that the full empirical cycle usually cannot be run repeatedly and typically prediction (often a key element of an empirical cycle) is impossible which implies that errors and imprecisions of initial assessments may not be corrected. Also considerable hysteresis exists with respect to the priors, in particular if a well-established theoretical framework and a coherent policy recipe existed before the event or if these priors are formulated strongly by intellectual and political leaders or leading institutions. Hysteresis in analysis and policy offers an additional possible explanation for the length of the long wave. Before a new paradigm can set in, the older generation has to be converted or perish (Kuhn 1972, p. 152).

12.2   DOES THE LONG WAVE MAKE SENSE?

The long wave hypothesis is, to say the least, not acceptable for everybody. One reason for its lack of popularity in science is probably that the hypothesis of the long wave is practical and empirical with low if any theoretical justification. Another reason is that explanations of the long wave often use non economic shocks, including war and peace, psychological mass moods, etc. Most economists recognize that such factors are important, but they find it difficult to see why these events should occur regularly with a more or less constant frequency. If 'economic fluctuations are irregular and unpredictable' as for example Mankiw (2008, p. 740) claims, why do the proponents of the long wave theories continue to see and interpret the evidence differently? (And note from the earlier quote that Kondratieff himself was not as outspoken as many modern day believers in 'his' wave.)

A Pattern Recognizing Species

The first reason is that humans are a pattern recognizing species. Our survival is based on the fact that we can very quickly see and recognize (ir)regularities. This is of tremendous help in daily life, but the capability comes at a cost because humans see patterns also when the patterns are absent. Consider for example Figure 12.1.

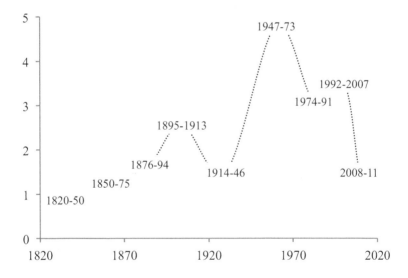

Sources: Korotayev and Tsirel, 2010, Tables 3 and 4 and IMF World Economic
          Outlook database, April 2012

*Figure 12.1   Average growth rates of real GPP in per cent during identified
           phases in Kondratieff cycles 1820 – 2011*

With some good will you can see a wave in these data, but not in the 19th century and not with a constant frequency and amplitude. Still this is the best evidence available...

Coincidence and Randomness

The second reason for the survival of the long wave hypothesis is that people have difficulty in coping with randomness and coincidence and do not sufficiently appreciate that important events simply happen by chance and not by design. Strange and seemingly significant results can and often do happen by chance due to the law of small numbers (Kahneman 2011, Chapter 10). Indeed, although the historical material from which the long wave is to be detected spans two centuries it is a very small sample since we have only five identified waves so far.

Perhaps in two centuries' time (when the sample period has been doubled) confirmation or falsification of the long wave hypothesis can be achieved, but for now it is a narrative that tells us that long periods of prosperity and growth are followed by downturns. The financial crisis that sparked the Great Recession may have been one of those turning points (but history will tell).

12.3   LIMITS TO GROWTH

The end of the two most recent cycles of the long wave is located at 1973 and 2007, years in which prices of raw materials and energy increased substantially reflecting unsustainable rates of exponential economic growth. This suggests that emerging scarcities and threats to the environment may have caused the downturn.

Indeed, scientists had realized that exponential growth processes were creating environmental problems and influential studies were published just before the downturn set in. In the 1970s *The Limits to Growth* (Meadows et al. 1972) preceded the first oil crisis and the breakdown of the Bretton Woods system of fixed exchange rates, in the 2000s *The Economics of Climate Change* (Stern, 2006) was published amidst price spikes in raw materials, food and energy and the financial crisis. Both studies clarified that exponential growth is not environmentally sustainable.

It is by no means accidental that studies on the environmental dangers of exponential economic growth appear in the run-up to a system breakdown. Typically in biological processes exponential growth eventually leads to collapse and extinction and *homo sapiens* cannot bend nature in this respect. It is, however, difficult to recognize that one is entering the danger zone if the process is exponential, so scientific studies with a high policy impact will tend to appear only at a later stage in the exponential growth process.

The studies by Meadows et al. and Stern are, however, more than symptoms as these studies clarify that exponential economic processes cannot continue, because they destruct our environment. There are two implications: (*i*) we have to rethink global growth (and probably at the Earth level that means zero growth and substantial redistribution between the present haves and have nots) and (*ii*) we cannot leave the environment to the market because firms and consumers do not consider the external effects of production and consumption when they make decisions. We need a government to remedy this market failure and since the environment is a global problem we need a global government.

Text Box 12.1 Exponential growth

Exponential growth is growth that occurs at a positive annual percentage, so that the accrual increases over time. Many economic variables grow over long periods, including GPP and population. Exponential growth of a variable implies that the value of the variable doubles approximately every $70/r$ periods, where r is the growth rate of the variable per period in per cent (so a growth rate of 3.5% per month means that the variable doubles in 20 months). This rule of thumb follows from the fact that if we want to double something at a growth rate of ρ and we want to find out how long that will take we need to solve $(1 + \rho)^T = 2$. (And if you want to find out how long it takes to triple simply solve $(1 + \rho)^T = 3$.) This means solving $T = \ln(2)/\ln(1+\rho)$ which for small values of ρ can be approximated by $\ln(2)/\rho$ or approximately $0.7/\rho$ and if you express ρ as a percentage you get the $70/r$ rule for the doubling time.

To see how this works, let us start with Adam and Eve and assume that population doubles every generation of 30 years. After 30 years we have 4 humans, after 60 years 8 humans, after 90 years 16 humans, etc. It takes 5 centuries to have a population of 100,000 but only an additional 1½ centuries to reach 1 million. Again 1½ centuries later 250 million people inhabit Earth. Nine centuries after Adam and Eve we have a population of 2150 million, 30 years later world population reaches 4300 million and only ten years later the 7 billion mark (the world population in 2011) is passed. It takes only 940 years to reach 7 billion, and importantly the last generation produces half the population (a corollary is that the amount of presently living people is almost equal to all people that have died on Earth).

It is the doubling that eventually causes the problem with exponential growth. It is difficult to note that one is operating in the danger zone. Daly (1992, p. 23) wonders

> Why has this transformation from a world relatively empty of human beings and manmade capital to a world relatively full of these not been noticed by economists? If such a fundamental change in the pattern of scarcity is real (...) then how could it be overlooked by economists whose job [it] is to pay attention to the pattern of scarcity.

According to Daly (1992, p. 24) this is due to the fact that exponential growth in the final phase moves faster than 'the speed with which fundamental economic paradigms shift'.

Exercise 12.1 Exponential growth

According to the UN's 2012 *Report on the Millennium Development Goals* in 2010, the share of people living on less than $1.25 a day dropped to less than half of its 1990 value. This means that MDG 1 – cutting the extreme poverty rate to half its 1990 level – has been achieved at the global level, well ahead of 2015.

- What is the annual growth rate by which the share of the global poor is dropping?

Care for the environment is not the only global public good that Earth needs for sustainability. Health, education, equality, justice, financial stability, peace and security are equally important for survival of the human species and have global dimensions (Kaul et al., 2003). Can we expect that forms of global governance will be available to provide these essential global public goods? Let us move to the next Part.

12.4   KEY CONCEPTS

- Black Swan
- Exponential growth
- External effect
- Juglar wave

- Kitchin wave
- Kuznets wave
- Kondratieff wave
- Market failure

PART III

EARTH GOVERNANCE AND GLOBAL PUBLIC
GOODS

13.   Global Public Goods

In this Part we will depart from the key abstraction of *Earth Economics* and look at some of the implications of the fact that people have always organized themselves at lower levels of aggregation than at the planetary level. People typically view themselves as being part of a nation, region or city and not (yet) as inhabitants of a specific planet. The practical way forward to making decisions at the planetary level has therefore always been through the cooperation of lower level aggregates. Actually that is also what happened earlier in history when nation states were built. Cities cooperated and became regions. Regions cooperated and became countries. Typically, lower transportation costs, easier communication and travel over longer distances and greater mobility increased the level at which cooperation was sought and achieved. An optimistic idealist would therefore probably stress that post Second World War cooperation increased substantially with many supranational forms of international cooperation. A rational realist would, however, point out that the power play of nations is here to stay, that collective global action is difficult to organize and that global public goods are undersupplied.

In this chapter I will give the floor to the realist approach. The key question that we will study is how the economic conditions for the demand and supply of global public goods have developed over time (and in Chapter 14 we will try to glean a bit into the future). I do so for two reasons: public goods are essential for the functioning of any economy (so also for Earth) and a global financial-economic policy is a global public good in itself. The three most important issues that we have to address are:

- The increasing demand for global public goods due to globalization and the emergence of truly global external effects.
- The impact on the supply of global public goods exerted by the relatively recent economic rise of large and populous nations, which are now considered to be the engines of global growth.
- The content, norms and values embedded in global public goods.

These issues are obviously interrelated. The wave of globalization that started in the mid 1990s is driven by the successful participation of the previous outs (centrally planned economies, many developing economies) in the Earth economy. It is difficult to conceive that the entailing shift in relative economic power will not translate into a shift in the politics of international governance and indeed one does not have to be a Marxist to expect a change in the norms and values in the global economic system. The non-OECD perspective is not anti-capitalistic *per se*, but typically gives more weight to coordination and the long-run effects of policies than in the industrialized countries that essentially still favour the atomistic individual freedom to choose (we will return to this issue in the next chapter). The probability of a change in the basic norms and values in world economic governance is especially probable since it will be more difficult for the OECD economies to continue to exercise their monopoly on global leadership with the emerging competitive fringe of China, Brazil, India and the likes.

Global Public Things

Earth's economy cannot flourish without global public goods, including non-economic goods and services such as human health care, the environment, universal education and peace. Likewise global public bads are a threat to Earth's economy: pandemics, climate change, financial instability and widespread poverty are clear examples. The Global Public Thing is typified by three characteristics:

- The Global Public Thing cannot be made excludable: if it is there it is available and unavoidable to all; consumers and users can neither be made to pay for the global public good nor escape from the global public bad (or only at extremely high costs).
- The consumption and use of the Global Public Thing is non-rival in the sense that consumption of additional units by others does not increase the costs of providing the good or bad (or the additional costs are near zero). Alternatively this does not reduce the quantity available to others.
- The Global Public Thing does not discriminate by nationality and cannot be stopped by borders.

Global public goods include global rules and regulations that are highly important for the proper functioning of the Earth economy. Examples are the rules against economic discrimination provided by the World Trade Organization (see http://www.wto.org/english/docs_e/legal_e/04-wto_e.htm), the labour standards provided by the International Labour Organization (see http://www.ilo.org/global/standards/lang--en/index.htm) and the health and food safety requirements set by the World Health Organization and the Food and Agriculture Organization. The Security Council of the United Nations sets political norms and values backed up by economic sanctions and peace-keeping missions. These forms of governance are important facilitators if not drivers for global economic cooperation and the global division of labour.

Clearly such global public goods do not develop in a void, but are the consequences of negotiation, compromise and cost sharing between nations. Sometimes global public goods come about spontaneously when countries, motivated by national considerations, move in the same direction as in the case of the global response to the Great Recession that we discussed in Chapter 6. Sometimes global public goods are provided by non governmental organizations that can both be commercial and non-profit; the Bank Identifier Code provided by the Society for Worldwide Interbank Financial Telecommunication (SWIFT) and your IP (internet address) provided by the Internet Corporation for Assigned Names and Numbers (ICANN) are examples of public goods that are essential facilities for the proper functioning of the world economy. While spontaneous and non governmental provision is thus possible, most often concerted action by governments is necessary to make progress.

The Provision of Global Public Goods: Collective Action Revisited

Mancur Olson's (1965 and 1982) theory of collective action is still one of the main references on the provision of public goods and the mechanism of cooperation between governments. Olson argued that collective action is plagued by the free rider problem. If the public good is provided then rational selfish beneficiaries that cannot be excluded from its use have no incentive to share in the costs of its provision. Why pay for something that you will get anyhow? The upshot is that only small and coherent groups can and will effectively engage in collective action (provided that it is mutually beneficial), but if the proceeds are to be divided by (too) many and cannot be substantially appropriated by the key producer then public goods will typically be underprovided. This chapter applies this analysis to cooperation at the global level. Charles Kindleberger (1986, p.2) pointed out that the

> tendency for public goods to be underproduced is serious enough within a nation bound by some sort of social contract, and directed in public matters by a government with the power to impose and collect taxes. It is (…) a more serious problem in international political and economic relations in the absence of international government.

All countries have an incentive to free ride and Kindleberger (1981, 1986) therefore argues that global public goods will only be produced by a hegemon (or leading nation) with sufficient clout both to initiate and to maintain the norms, values, standards, etc. that underpin the working of the Earth economy. In this view a natural candidate for judging the possibilities for public good provision is the share in the benefits that a leading country or group of countries can expect from providing the global public good. Indeed, Sandler (1998) identifies a small number of essential countries and the presence of an influential leader as prerequisites for supranational collective action. In short, if the share of the hegemon or the leading group in GPP is low, the public good is less likely to be produced. The motivation is straightforward. If the public good is necessary for production then it follows directly that the benefits are proportional to the share in GPP and if the benefits that can be derived depend on economic or market power, then the share in GPP is also relevant as an indicator of economic dominance. Note that this argument differs from the traditional interpretation that it is the group size that makes the provision of global public goods difficult; it is not only the size but also the fragmentation of the group that matters. Before we analyse the development of global fragmentation as one of the supply conditions for global public good provision we first take a look at the demand side.

13.1 GLOBALIZATION

The concept of globalization passes the elephant test: 'difficult to describe but you know what it is when you see one'. Terrabites have by now been spent on defining globalization and I will not even attempt to come up with my own definition, but follow a practical course. Globalization is about increasing interaction with citizens, firms, non-governmental organizations and governments in *other* countries. Interaction can be social, economic or political. Figure 13.2 uses the so-called KOF Index of Globalization (Dreher, 2006) to illustrate the development of these three different aspects of globalization (the total globalization index combines these measures):

- Economic globalization: a measure based on actual flows (trade and foreign investment openness) as well as restrictions (such as hidden import barriers and capital restrictions).
- Social globalization: a measure that takes into account the extent and intensity of personal contact of earthlings on different sides of borders (including international telephone calls and letters, tourism), the

international composition of population, information flows (internet, television, foreign newspapers) and cultural proximity.
- Political globalization: a measure based on the network of embassies, membership in international organizations, participation in U.N. Security Council missions and the number of conducted international treaties. This measure indicates the extent (density) of political integration into global decision-making networks.

All components of globalization have shown a considerable increase since the 1970s with 1990 acting as an important inflexion point, not only because of the breakdown of the Soviet Union and the Iron Curtain but also because Second and Third World countries increasingly participate in international organizations, treaties and expand their international diplomatic networks (if this interests you, consult van Bergeijk 2009). Even recently, while – due to the Great Recession – economic globalization is witnessing an actual downturn and social globalization became stagnant, political globalization continues on a clear upward trend.

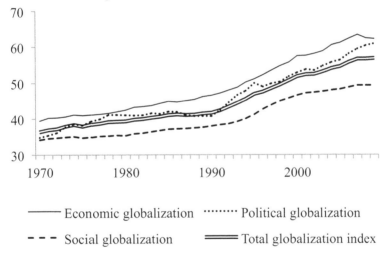

Source: http://globalization.kof.ethz.ch, accessed July 2012

Figure 13.1 KOF index of globalization, 1970 – 2009

The steady upward trend in political globalization probably reflects that economic interaction generates external cross-border effects. Trade and capital flows increasingly link economies so that the economic policies of one country influence the economic health of other countries. Migration and tourism spread knowledge about other political, economic and environmental systems, but also increase security risks. People and products spread knowledge, ideas, lifestyles and diseases alike.

Exercise 13.1 Globalization
- Read the following two texts.
- When do you think that these texts were written?

Text 1
[He] could order by telephone, sipping his morning tea in bed, the various products of the whole earth, in such quantity as he might see fit, and reasonably expect their early delivery upon his doorstep; he could at the same moment and by the same means adventure his wealth in the natural resources and new enterprises of any quarter of the world, and share, without exertion or even trouble, in their prospective fruits and advantages; or he could decide to couple the security of his fortunes with the good faith of the townspeople of any substantial municipality in any continent that fancy or information might recommend. He could secure forthwith, if he wished it, cheap and comfortable means of transit to any country or climate without passport or other formality, (...) and could then proceed abroad to foreign quarters, without knowledge of their religion, language, or customs, (...), and would consider himself greatly aggrieved and much surprised at the least interference. But, most important of all, he regarded this state of affairs as normal, certain, and permanent.

Text 2
Modern industry has established the world market (... which gave) an immense development to commerce, to navigation, to communication. This development has, in turn, reacted on the extension of industry. The need of a constantly expanding market for its products chases [it] over the entire surface of the globe. It must nestle everywhere, settle everywhere, establish connections everywhere. It has given a cosmopolitan character to production and consumption in every country. (...) it has drawn from under the feet of industry the national ground on which it stood. All old-established national industries have been destroyed or are daily being destroyed. They are dislodged by new industries, whose introduction becomes a life and death question for all civilized nations, by industries that no longer work up indigenous raw material, but raw material drawn from the remotest zones; industries whose products are consumed, not only at home, but in every quarter of the globe. In place of the old wants, satisfied by the production of the country, we find new wants, requiring for their satisfaction the products of distant lands and climes. In place of the old local and national seclusion and self-sufficiency, we have intercourse in every direction, universal inter-dependence of nations.

Borders of course remain important (and the economic influence of borders is still high) but like the plasma membrane borders have become semi-permeable and cannot protect against all outside threats. Prevention thus requires reducing the outside threat levels and this provides the incentive to invest in political cooperation. Globalization, while fuelling the demand for global public goods, also depends on open trading systems, free high seas, property rights, standards and peace – in short: global public goods are engines for globalization too.

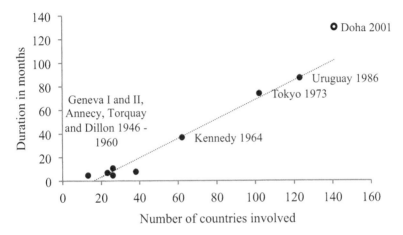

Figure 13.2   Costs in terms of duration of increased participation in multilateral trade negotiations (GATT and WTO, 1946 – present)

The increased participation of countries in the global political and economic system comes, however, at a cost as is illustrated in Figure 13.2 for the case of the post Second World War multilateral trade negotiation rounds. The early rounds involved 34 countries at most and all were finished within the year. The Uruguay round that started in 1986 with 123 countries took 87 months. The Doha round started in 2001 with 141 countries (and when this book went to the printers already 134 months had passed). Although it is true that the rounds have become more complex over time covering many more items and issues than earlier rounds, Figure 13.2 illustrates that international collective action becomes more difficult when the number of countries is large. The history of the WTO itself is also highly instructive. It actually took the world community five decades to create the organization foreseen at Bretton Woods in 1944. This is not an exceptionally long period for the creation of global institutions: the creation of the World Health Organization, for example, required eight decades.

13.2 GLOBAL EXTERNAL EFFECTS

Global external effects are effects of economic activities that impact the globe. In order to tackle these effects global collective action is necessary. Why have these problems become more important? In finding an answer, let us take an even longer perspective than developed in Part II and go back to the year 250,000 BC, just before *homo sapiens* enters the scene. It is easy to see that many things that are now considered to be global public goods were available at that time: sunlight, moonlight, fresh air, biodiversity, waterways, the high seas, etc. There was even more that could be consumed without rivalry: the fruits of nature, game, land, etc. Now enters *homo sapiens*: human design and social construct invent ownership and assign property rights to what was once free for all. Human creativity still has not been able to develop a business model to exploit all Earth's public goods, but it is clear that a lot has changed, as markets now exist for many of these goods that were moved to the private realm. Population density was the principal driver for the emergence of property rights and markets. Consumption and use became rival when population increased. The same development, however, also drove the emergence of governance and the need for public good provision, because the property rights had to be registered, accepted and defended. The lesson here is that public and private goods are social constructs that move in tandem, while the decision of what is produced in the private and the public realm depends on conditions of time and place.

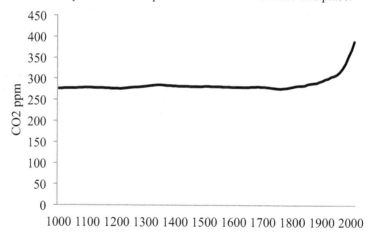

Source: www.climexp.knmi.nl, accessed July 2012

Figure 13.3 Atmospheric carbon dioxide concentration 1000 – 2010 in ppm

This is a process that continues as of today, because the growth of population and production now threatens other global public goods including the atmosphere. Figure 13.3 shows how the industrial revolution generated unprecedented atmospheric change. The ensuing global warming generated collective action that also involves new markets for emission trading, illustrating again that both public and private actors have a role to play in the provision of global public goods. It is, however, not only population and production density that have created global external effects. New technologies also have increased risks of global disasters. The fall-out of nuclear weapons and nuclear accidents and the greater ease of travel for viruses and diseases (by car, train, ship and plane) are examples. Like globalization, global external effects are drivers of the demand for institutions and rules and regulations that can contain or prevent global public bads.

13.3   FRAGMENTATION AND LEADERSHIP: HISTORY

For long parts of history global cooperation was not necessary. Empires were built and alliances were created, but their impact did not extend to the global level. The Roman Empire covered Europe and Northern Africa, but did not reach into the Americas and Asia. The onset of globalization by the Great Discoveries brought misery and exploitation to large parts of the world, but those problems were geographically limited and did not threaten the human species as a whole.

This changed with the rise of modern capitalism and imperialism that coincided with the building of the British Empire that spanned the world. This development ultimately brought the waves of self-destructive behaviour that are characteristic of our species to the truly global level culminating in the First World War. The governments of the time responded to that wake-up call and created the League of Nations, but did not yet sufficiently recognize the crucial importance of underlying economic conditions, and were unable to solve by collective actions the problems of, first, the Great Depression and, later, the rise to economic and military power of Germany, Italy and Japan, that felt deprived of their rights to expand.

The experiences of the two World Wars were strong motivators for the new hegemon, the United States of America, for the creation of the United Nations and the Bretton Woods institutions (International Monetary Fund, World Bank and the General Agreement on Tariffs and Trade that became the World Trade Organization in 1995). War prone Europe helped by the Marshall Plan started a process of regional economic and political cooperation with the creation of the European Economic Community in

1957, the European Union in 1993 and a common currency (the euro) in 1999 as important milestones and outstanding examples of supranational cooperation.

In the 1990s two qualitative changes in the global political and economic system occurred that both enabled global cooperation and enhanced the need for planetary decision-making. The major political factor was the end of the superpower conflict and the breakdown of the Soviet Union. The economic counterpart is the new phase in globalization that became broadly based and increased in speed and intensity (as illustrated in Figure 13.1).

Measurement

Figure 13.4 provides a numerical long-term perspective on the development of economic power in the global system, that – as discussed earlier – is an important determinant of the likelihood of global public good provision. The basis of observation is the nation state (so for example the countries of the European Union are included on an individual basis since the United States of Europe, foreseen by Winston Churchill in 1946, is still not a reality).

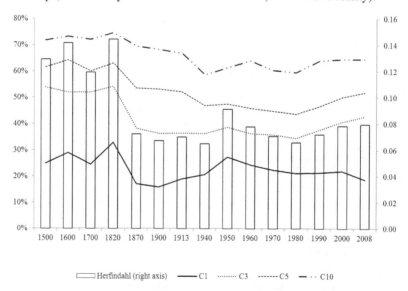

Source: Calculations based on Maddison's historical data series

Figure 13.4 Concentration in the world economy 1500 – 2008

Figure 13.4 reports a number of key statistics that have been developed in industrial economics to measure market power (that is: the power to influence the market outcome).

The first set of concentration measures are reported in the form of so-called C_N – concentration ratios that are defined as the share in GPP of the N biggest producing countries (I use N = 1, 3, 5 or 10, so a range that runs from 1 (for the single largest country or hegemon) to 10 (the share of the ten largest countries, say the G10 of the time)). The most dynamic power shifts occur for the largest country as shown by the C_1. This is of course not the same country in all periods: before the 20th century China consistently had the largest share in GPP.

The advent of new hegemons is reflected in a higher value for the second indicator, the Herfindahl index because the dominant country is contested by a power that grows equally large in share of GPP. The Herfindahl index is defined as the sum of the squared shares. In this case the share Ω_i is the GDP of country i in per cent of GPP. The Herfindahl index equals $\sum \Omega_i^2$. If there is one producer the Herfindahl index is 1 and if production is fully atomistic the Herfindahl index approaches 0.

Figure 13.4 illustrates that fragmentation has been relatively high since the industrial revolution. After 1870 the Herfindahl index has values that are characteristic for situations with many players and a market outcome that is 'competitive'. The advent of British hegemony is reflected in a higher Herfindahl index, because the dominant country is contested. By 1870 concentration and potential for dominance have decayed. The end of the Second World War brings US hegemony and the Herfindahl index increases again, but in the 1960s decay sets in. The Herfindahl index bottoms out in the 1980s reflecting stronger growth in the periphery, in particular of China, suggesting the advent of a new hegemon. (Note that the data series ends in 2008 just before the crisis and thus misses the fact that the OECD experienced negative growth while China stayed in positive territory.)

Exercise 13.2 Fragmentation
- Collect country GDPs at current prices and in US$ starting in 1995 until as recent as possible from the IMF World Economic Outlook Database (see exercise 3.5 but chose 'by country').
- Calculate country shares in GPP.
- Calculate the Herfindahl index.
- Compare your results for the years 2000 and 2008 with Figure 13.4 and explain the differences.

Implications

Recently policy makers have started to pay a lot of attention to the occurrence of multipolarity and its implications. The World Bank (2011a) study *Global Development Horizons 2011: Multipolarity - The New Global Economy* is a clear example. One finding is that the concentration of global growth has substantially decreased since the 1970s when the Herfindahl index was 0.21 (the 2008 figure is 0.08; see Lin and Rosenblatt 2012, p. 24). Unlike the World Bank study this chapter focuses on shares derived from levels (rather than from growth rates), because the share of the leading economies in GPP is the determinant of global public good provision. Taking a longer time perspective, the key issue is not multipolarity but hegemony. Perhaps an alternative for hegemony can be developed if a small group of leading economies can work closely together to provide the necessary governance and global public goods. The next chapter investigates that option.

13.4   KEY CONCEPTS

- Collective action
- Excludable
- Fragmentation
- G20
- Globalization
- Global public bads
- Global public goods

- Hegemon
- Non-rival
- Herfindahl index
- Property rights
- Rival
- Supranational

14. Global Peers: An Agenda

Global governance is in a tremendous flux. The financial crisis, the world trade collapse and the run-a-way public debt problems may be symptoms of a fundamental change in the division of economic power and reflect growing and unsustainable imbalances and increasing complexity of the international networks of nations, firms and citizens. The governance of the international system and the relationships between independent states are changing substantively and at an unprecedented speed. The financial crisis has revealed the costs of an absent overarching authority and this lack of effective governance is the inspiration for change that has led to an upgrading of the G20. In view of the previous chapter this may seem to be a step backward because we saw that the provision of global public goods such as the governance of the economic and financial system is best served by a small group of countries. This argument would seem to favour the G8 over the G20, but actually the G20 is an appropriate response to the success of the emerging markets and the disappointing performance of the rich countries. This is especially true in view of the still large political, economic and cultural differences between the countries that presently grow and the countries that stagnate – between the previous outs and the still ins. Some argue that the shift in economic power endangers the open multilateral systems that govern trade, finance and the division of labour.

New Entrants

A critical question is why the rise of the emerging economies is seen as problematic at all since the world economic system absorbed several waves of new entrants since the Second World War. Those waves did not challenge the basic underpinnings of global economic governance. The integration of the war prone economies in Western Europe led to a stronger economic power base. The re-emergence of Japan as an important economic power and the subsequent advent of the Newly Industrializing Economies (the so-called Asian Tigers) in the 1970s and 1980s did not constitute a threat to the governing paradigm of multilateralism and markets, essentially because the new entrants embraced those principles. Likewise the 1989 fall of the Iron

161

Curtain and the Soviet Union's breakdown actually strengthened the domination of market-oriented policies. So why would this time be different?

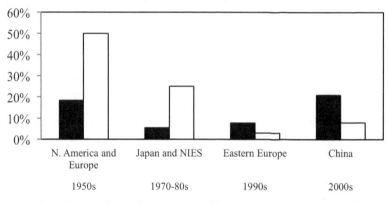

Sources: US census bureau and World Bank development indicators

Figure 14.1   Population and production shares of key players at the start of the waves of global integration (1950s – 2000s)

Figure 14.1 illustrates that the difference does not follow from the production share of the new entrants at the start of the wave (although the increase in China's global production share over the last decade has been spectacular). The challenge that China and India pose to the world economic system follows from the size of their populations (and thus from their potential production shares). Indeed, within a decade the BRIICs country group (Brazil, Russia, India, Indonesia and China) may have a global majority share in terms of *both* population and production and this will constitute a powerful and hard to ignore base for rightful demands to change governance and the direction of the world economic institutions.

Multi What?

The problem is that too many international institutions exist that do not yet involve these countries in their deliberations because they are not yet full-fledged modern market economies. In the Organisation for Economic Co-operation and Development, for example, membership talks have only started with Russia, while Brazil, India and China have only been offered 'enhanced engagement', which is quite distinct from accession to that organization. In practical terms this means that these countries are formally not allowed at the table when global economic, social and environmental policies are discussed.

The G8 in the past typically offered the Heads of State of China, Brazil and India a photo opportunity only but no real participation in the deliberations. The secretaries-general, chair persons and presidents of the major international institutions are still "by tradition" from the OECD countries (most often Europe and the United States).

Diagram 14.1   Multi-polar (left), multi-system (middle) and multi-lateral (right) governance

It is increasingly being recognized that significant poles of growth are emerging outside the traditional economic powers and their allies. Global governance in a multi-polar system requires that small states align with large states while the poles in the system basically compete (although co-ordination and cooperation are possible of course). The left-hand panel of Diagram 14.1 illustrates this usual format for monetary, fiscal and exchange rate policies (the circles represent countries). *De facto* the multi-polar world that many observers see developing, however, is a multi system world because many important countries are not included in the formal global decision-making institutions (middle panel Diagram 14.1). Consequently, regional governance systems are developing that compete with (multilateral) forms of global governance. Thus we have seen, for example, regional initiatives to organize regional alternatives to the IMF and the World Bank. A particularly worrisome scenario is that power is not (or too slowly) handed over to the big emerging economies so that they will work towards different forms of global governance with other norms, values and rules. The key challenge is to accept the emerging countries as peers and strengthen the legitimacy of global governance. But what are the prospects for global governance in a world that gets more and more fragmented?

14.1 FRAGMENTATION AND LEADERSHIP: FUTURE

Let us again take a long-term perspective (but this time we will move into the future) using the Great Shift study (Fouré et al., 2012) of the Centre d'Études Prospectives et d'Informations Internationales (CEPII) that deploys the

MaGE model (Macroeconometrics of the Global Economy). Figure 14.2 takes an optimistic view on current and future fragmentation as it treats the 27 countries that constitute the European Union as one state. Technically this reduces the extent of measured fragmentation compared to the data reported in Figure 13.4 as it builds a new second world pole. The C_3 ratio in 2010 according to this measure is 63%.

Exercise 14.1 Comparing fragmentation
- Compare the level of the Herfindahl index and the C_3 ratio in Figure 13.4 and Figure 14.2.

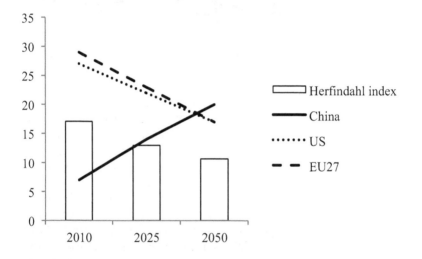

Source: Calculations based on Fouré et al. (2012), p.57.

Figure 14.2 GPP shares of China, EU27 and the United States and Herfindahl index of the Earth economy 2010 – 2050

Figure 14.2, however, is also quite realistic as it takes feedback mechanisms into account and goes beyond simple extrapolation of existing trends (China's current growth rate of 8% per annum would, for example, result in a 21 fold increase in GDP by 2050; in the MaGe model the increase is 'only' 8-fold). According to Figure 14.1 the outlook for the provision of global public goods and thus of global governance provides several challenges. Firstly, the trend is towards greater fragmentation as shown by the Herfindahl index. The C_3-ratio that measures the market share of the three largest economies decreases from 63% in 2010 to 54% in 2050. (Note that the future downward trend in the C_3-ratio contrasts with the improvement since the 1980s reported in Figure 13.4). (This fragmentation is also good news for many people because it reflects the improvement of their standards of living due to the catching-up of the large emerging economies.) Secondly, China becomes the largest economy by 2050, but its share in 2050 GPP is lower than the current share in GPP of the present hegemon, the United States.

The increased fragmentation of the international power structure that is moving from a (bi)polar system dominated by the US and Europe towards a less concentrated system suggests that the current phase is crucial: if the three largest economies can cooperate they have a window of opportunity to build and strengthen global governance (see, for example, Bénassy-Quéré and Pisani-Ferry 2012 with regards to challenges of the global financial system). That window, however, is likely to close around 2050 when the C_3-ratio decays and the then hegemon China will have less clout than during previous episodes. The year 2050 seems to be far away and to leave ample scope for action. The longevity of the process of international institution building (that, as we saw in the previous chapter, often takes many decades) actually implies that action is urgently needed.

The legitimacy of global institutions can ultimately be based on two principles: (*i*) the representation of nation states in a multilateral system and (*ii*) the principle of representation on the basis of one earthling one vote.

Multilateralism

If Earth opts for the multilateral system then the industrialized world should not alienate China and other emerging economic powers from that system, but involve them right now. First of all, this implies that rather than simply imposing Western norms and values one should respect the difficulties and choices underlying the Chinese development model and its apparent success. Rather than applying the accession rules to get copycats of the industrialized nations the emerging economic powers should be accepted as peers. The industrialized nations should already now literally make room at the tables of the international decision-making institutions.

Multilateralism – as it is about cooperation between nation states – may, however, encounter problems due to globalization that has extended the informal and formal networks of all actors and accordingly made them both more influential and more vulnerable with regard to behaviour in other jurisdictions. Even actors with geographically limited direct networks and activities (so actors that remain in the purely domestic or national realms such as the butcher and the baker) have increasingly become linked across borders through upstream or downstream activities in their formal and informal networks and through the internationalization of the activities of other nearby actors.

The increasing importance of activity that goes beyond borders (that is: beyond the geographic location of the State) has substantial implications for the State as its stakeholders get fragmented across jurisdictions. Traditionally the State had to deal only with its own citizens as they constitute the franchise, but due to the cross border linkages non-state actors in other jurisdictions (including multinational enterprises, consumer organizations and protester movements) can influence the State and its interactions with other States and thus need further reconsideration. Rodrik's (2000) political trilemma for the word economy studies the interaction of states and franchise in the context of globalization: Earth cannot maintain at the same time international economic integration, the nation-state and mass politics (i.e. unrestricted franchise, political mobilization and responsive political institutions). If Rodrik is right, then the nation state may have to give in.

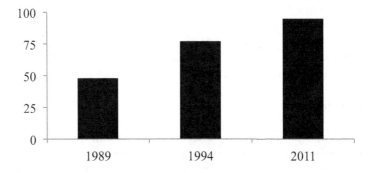

Source: Marshall and Cole (2011)

Figure 14.3 Number of democracies worldwide, 1989 – 2011

Proportional Representation

The above implies that Earth should perhaps work towards a better and proportional representation of earthlings. World government based on the one earthling, one vote principle is still seen as an idealistic principle rather than a concrete realist option. Still, as Marhall and Cole (2011, p.10) note, Earth since the 1990s is definitely on a path towards a much more democratic context:

> The one thing that most clearly distinguishes the Globalization Era is that, for the first time in human history, the global system is predominantly comprised of independent states and populated by democratic regimes.

Also in view of the emerging political trilemma and the fragmentation of the State's stakeholders across jurisdictions one might reconsider multilateralism rather than proportional representation as the idealistic principle. Earth should take courage from Churchill's observation in 1947:

> Many forms of Government have been tried and will be tried in this world of sin and woe. No one pretends that democracy is perfect or all-wise. Indeed, it has been said that democracy is the worst form of government except all those other forms that have been tried from time to time.

The realist may want to point out that vested interested will oppose the entailing shift of economic and political power. Economists, however, have a long and emancipatory tradition of fighting overstretched and out-dated concepts of governance:

> They are founded upon the most absurd of all suppositions, the supposition that every successive generation of men have not an equal right to the earth, and to all that it possesses; but that the property of the present generation should be restrained and regulated according to the fancy of those who died perhaps five hundred years ago (Smith 1776, II.2.6).

Whatever course Earth takes, it is clear that the ideas, preferences and right-full demands of all earthlings should be represented on an equal footing in the governance of the planet.

14.2 A GLOBAL AGENDA OF PEERS

The global agenda should no longer start in the global North. For long development aid has been modelled as a look-a-like of the Marshall Plan for the recovery of the European nations after the Second World War. Likewise the Washington Consensus prescribed free markets and small government because that seemed to work in the industrialized countries. Many indications exist that one should be critical about the wisdom and general validity of the policy prescriptions that come from the developed countries, ranging from the lack of progress for the Least Developed Countries (Fialho, 2012) to the financial and economic crisis, that forced 'those who did not gain earlier to pay for the sins of irresponsible and unregulated finance' (Gosh 2011, p. 22).

Several authors have recognized the validity of ideas and economic concepts developed in the South. Lin and Rosenblatt (2012) have noted that most ideas about economics – even about development economics – have been developed in the industrialized countries. They call for a democratization of development economics

The economic theories that originate in developed countries attempt to explain and promote the growth in the developed countries; as such, they may not be relevant to developing countries because of the differences in the challenges and opportunities (…). Meanwhile, successful developing countries have generated many useful lessons for how to achieve dynamic growth. Their experiences will be more relevant for other developing countries than the experiences of the developed countries because of the similarity of their opportunities and challenges. Most economic theories are produced by economists in developed countries with the intention to explain economic phenomena in developed countries or by economists who use developed countries as reference to explain phenomena in developing countries (such as structuralism and the Washington Consensus). (…M)any economic and social constraints to development differ across countries and/or across time (Lin and Rosenblatt 2012, p. 35).

Van der Hoeven (2012) notes the exclusion of the global North from the Millennium Development Goals.

The geo-economic shifts force us to rethink the concept of development, poverty and the goals that the world will set itself in 2015. The crises of 2008, and the current challenges of the reduction of public and private debts caused by the financial crisis, make it very clear that protecting the poor and the socially disadvantaged in industrialized countries has also become a serious political and societal problem. One might, therefore, consider MDG targets for all countries including the developed countries. First, the growing globalization and greater interconnectedness is creating hardships also for socio-economic groups in developed countries, and it would be politically unwise to ignore this in a post-2015 system. Second, targets for all countries in a post-2015 system need to express better than in the current MDG system the continuing and shared responsibility of each country in our global world.

Earth's problems are becoming increasingly complex and of a cross border character. And so are Earth's solutions. Achieving solutions requires a new social contract. This is the challenge for us all: a global social contract between peers.

14.3   KEY CONCEPTS

- Millennium Development Goals
- Multi-lateral
- Multilateralism
- Multi-polar
- Multi-system
- One-earthling-one-vote
- Social contract

Answers to the Exercises

Exercise 2.1 UN National Accounts Database

This answer depends on your home country. You check the data availability at http://unstats.un.org/unsd/snaama/cList.asp. For my home country (Planet Earth which you will find under the label 'world') the most recent data available in October 2012 was the year 2010. The share of world final consumption in per cent of GPP was $ 48.4 trillion / 63.1 trillion billion = 76.7%. (Note that for your country you will have to use GDP rather than GPP and that you can do calculations in national currency as well as in dollars.)

Exercise 2.2 Contribution of economic activities

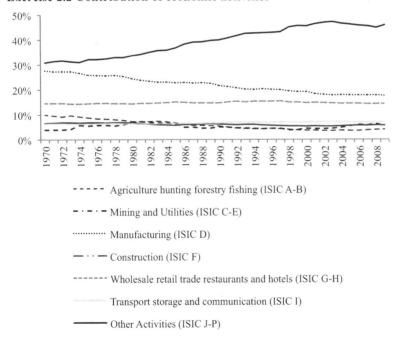

- - - - - Agriculture hunting forestry fishing (ISIC A-B)

- · - · - Mining and Utilities (ISIC C-E)

············ Manufacturing (ISIC D)

— · · — Construction (ISIC F)

- - - - - - Wholesale retail trade restaurants and hotels (ISIC G-H)

              Transport storage and communication (ISIC I)

—————— Other Activities (ISIC J-P)

Note that the latest data available for value added by activity was 2009, not 2010. The share of manufacturing in Planetary Product was 18 per cent in 2009.

Exercise 2.3 Construction of Planet Accounts

The matrix below summarizes the Planet Accounts and the relevant concepts and aggregates.

	MANUF	OTHER	*Total Interme-diate*	Final Consum-ption	Fixed Capital	In-ven-tory	Final De-mand	*Total Output*
MANUF	9	13	*22*	17	9	2	28	*50*
OTHER	11	1	*12*	19	4	0	23	*35*
Total Inter-mediate	*20*	*14*	*34*	*36*	*13*	*2*	*51*	*85*

			Total factor income
Wages	18	15	*33*
Rents	1	3	*4*
Interest	2	4	*6*
Profit	9	-1	*8*
Value added	30	21	*51*

Total inputs	*50*	*35*	*85*

Exercise 3.1 Growth rates

Year-on-year 2008/2007: 9.9%.
Year-on-year 2009/2008: – 5.6%.
Arithmetic average: (9.9 – 5.6)/2 = 4.3/2 = 2.2%.
Geometric average: 2009/2007: $\sqrt{(57.8/55.7)} - 1 = 1.9\%$.
The geometric average is the average increase in the level over 2007 – 2009; the arithmetic average is the average of the individual growth rates.

Exercise 3.2 Recovery

Recovery to previous level in 2010, but recovery to trend is not yet in sight; see the figure.

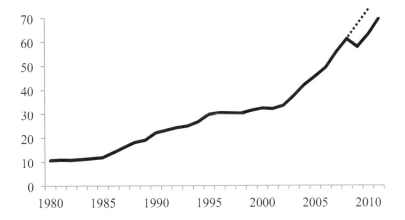

Exercise 3.3 Business cycle

Trough 1998, Peak 2000, Trough 2001.

Exercise 3.4 Inflation and real variables

Price level still increases but at lower pace.

	Inflation (GPP deflator)	GDP in constant prices of 2008	Real GDP gr
y-o-y 2007	8.5%	60.5	
y-o-y 2008	8.6%	61.2	1.2%
y-o-y 2009	−3.4%	59.8	−2.2%

Approximations: 2008: 9.9 − 8.6 = 1.3 and −5.6 + 3.4 = −2.2

Exercise 3.5 Prepare an up to date data set for the Earth economy

Answers to data set building exercises depend on the latest data sets made available by international organizations. In some cases the answers provided below are subject to revisions of these data sets as well. Consult the dedicated website http://www.eartheconomics.info.

Exercise 4.1 Marginal rate of consumption

- Otherwise you always spend more than you earn.
- If autonomous consumption C_0 equals zero.

Exercise 4.2 Consumption in the world economy

See: www.eartheconomics.info.

Exercise 4.3 Permanent income

This is a reduction in permanent income/expected future income and thus it will reduce current and future consumption.

Exercise 4.4 $I = S$ (Diagram 4.3)

In a point to the left of E planned investment would exceed planned saving so that inventories are run down in order to make planned consumption possible. Firms will increase production and the adjustment is to the right (large Y).

Exercise 4.5 Stability

Stable equilibrium

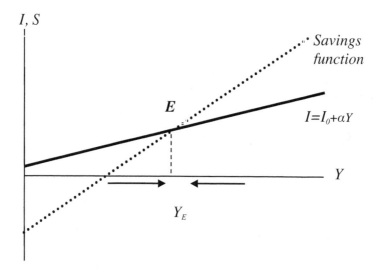

The equilibrium does not exist for $\alpha = (1 - c)$. For $\alpha < (1 - c)$ we have a stable equilibrium as illustrated by point E above. For $\alpha > (1 - c)$ the equilibrium is unstable as illustrated by point F below.

Unstable equilibrium

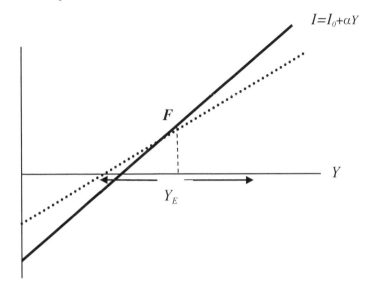

Exercise 4.6 Multiplier

See also Exercise 4.3. GPP decreases by 3.4 and investment by 2.1. The multiplier is about 1.6.

Exercise 5.1 Investment function

The NPV of the discounted cash flows is $-35 + \frac{10}{1+R} + \frac{10}{(1+R)^2} + \frac{10}{(1+R)^3} + \frac{10}{(1+R)^4}$
For $R = 0$ this becomes $-35+40=5$.

Exercise 5.2 Elasticity

Elasticities in (I,R) are: $(40,0)$: 0; $(24,4)$: $-^2/_3$; $(20,5)$: -1; $(8,8)$: -4; $(0,10)$: $-\infty$

Exercise 5.3 Reduced form equation

$S = Y - C = (1-c)Y - C_0$ and $Y = \frac{1}{1-c}(I_0 + C_0) - \frac{i}{1-c}R$

So that the reduced for equation for S is

$(1-c)\{\frac{1}{1-c}(I_0 + C_0) - \frac{i}{1-c}R\} - C_0 = I_0 - iR$

An increase in R reduces the equilibrium value of S

Exercise 5.4 Interest rate elasticity

For a vertical IS curve the interest rate elasticity is 0 because changes in R do not move Y. For a horizontal IS curve the interest rate elasticity is infinite: a small change in R leads to a very large change in Y.

Exercise 5.5 Shifting the IS curve

The curve shifts to the right.
$R = \frac{I_0 + C_0}{i} - \frac{1-c}{i} Y$: an increase in i shifts the curve down and makes it flatter.

Exercise 5.6 Autonomous spending and IS curve

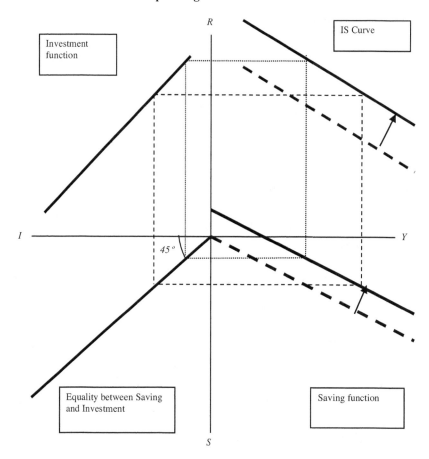

Exercise 6.1 Taxation

Income taxes are payable at $Y=T_0$.
A lump sum tax is a horizontal line at the level of the tax.
Proportional: average tax rate stays the same as income increases: $T/Y = t$.
Progressive: average tax rate increases as income increases: $T/Y = t - T_0/Y$.

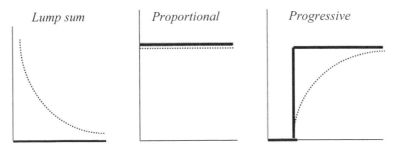

| Lump sum | Proportional | Progressive |

....Average rate of taxation ⎯ Marginal rate of taxation

Exercise 6.2 Taxation in the Model

Model with proportional taxation and exogenous government expenditure:

Consumption function:	$C_t = cY^D + C_0$	(1)
Definition equation:	$Y^D = Y - T$	(2)
Definition equation:	$S = Y - C$	(3)
Investment function:	$I = I_0 - iR$	(4)
Government spending function:	$G = G_0$	(5)
Tax function:	$T = tY$	(6)
Equilibrium equation:	$I + G = S + T$	(7)

Endogenous: Y, Y^D, C, I, S, T, G
Exogenous: $c, i, I_0, C_0, G_0, R, t$

Solve $I + G = S + T$ for Y; so set

$$I_0 - iR + G_0 = Y - C + T = Y - c(Y - tY) - C_0 = (1 - c)(1 - t)Y - C_0 + tY$$

in order to get the reduced form equation

$$Y = (I_0 + C_0 + G_0)/\{1 - c(1 - t)\} - iR/\{1 - c(1 - t)\} \qquad (8)$$

Note that the multiplier for exogenous spending components changes from $1/(1 - c)$ to $1/\{1 - c(1 - t)\}$ and this is a smaller multiplier. If, e.g., $c = 0.8$ and $t = 0.25$ the multiplier $1/(1 - c) = 1/0.2 = 5$ becomes $1/\{1 - c(1 - t)\} = 1/0.4 = 2.5$. The reason why the multiplier decreases should be clear by now: out of each extra unit of income 60% is consumed (15% is saved and 25% is paid in taxes) so that the multiplier becomes $1 + 0.6 + 0.6^2 + 0.6^3 + \ldots + 0.6^n = 2.5$.

Exercise 6.3 Inequality

The Gini coefficient is Area A/Area (A+B) or approximately 7/12.5=56%

Exercise 6.4 Asymmetry of taxes and subsidies

Add a component $+T_0$ to equation (15.6) so that the reduced form equation becomes:

$$Y = (I_0 + C_0 + G_0 - cT_0)/\{(1 - c(1 - t)\} - iR/\{1 - c(1 - t)\} \qquad (15.8')$$

The multiplier for a subsidy (one unit of G_0) is $1/\{1 - c(1 - t)\}$ and for one unit of extra taxation $-c/\{1 - c(1 - t)\}$ which is smaller in absolute size.

Exercise 6.5 Debt dynamics

Year	GPP	Taxation	Government spending	Primary deficit
2011	70.0	9.6	10.5	0.9
2012	73.9	10.2	11.1	0.9
2013	77.9	10.7	11.7	1.0
2014	82.2	11.3	12.3	1.0
2015	86.7	11.9	13.0	1.1
2016	91.5	12.6	13.7	1.1
2017	96.5	13.3	14.5	1.2

R=4,Ÿ=5.5	Interest	Deficit	Debt	Deficit/GPP	Debt/GPP
2011	2.2	3.1	56.0	4.5%	80%
2012	2.4	3.3	59.1	4.5%	80%
2013	2.5	3.5	62.4	4.5%	80%
2014	2.6	3.7	65.9	4.5%	80%
2015	2.8	3.9	69.5	4.5%	80%
2016	2.9	4.1	73.4	4.5%	80%
2017	3.1	4.3	77.5	4.5%	80%

In this simple model the central prognosis in the IMF World Economic Outlook data base is consistent with a stable Debt-to-GPP ratio and a constant deficit at this rate of growth and this interest rate.

R=5,Ÿ=5.5	Interest	Deficit	Debt	Deficit/GPP	Debt/GPP
2011	2.8	3.7	56.0	5.3%	80%
2012	3.0	3.9	59.7	5.3%	81%
2013	3.2	4.2	63.6	5.3%	82%
2014	3.4	4.4	67.7	5.4%	82%
2015	3.6	4.7	72.1	5.4%	83%
2016	3.8	5.0	76.8	5.4%	84%
2017	4.1	5.3	81.8	5.5%	85%

R=4,Ÿ=4.5	Interest	Deficit	Debt	Deficit/GPP	Debt/GPP
2011	2.2	3.1	56.0	4.5%	80%
2012	2.4	3.3	59.1	4.5%	81%
2013	2.5	3.5	62.4	4.5%	82%
2014	2.6	3.6	65.8	4.5%	82%
2015	2.8	3.8	69.5	4.6%	83%
2016	2.9	4.0	73.3	4.6%	84%
2017	3.1	4.2	77.3	4.6%	85%

Small deviations in interest and growth make the debt problem difficult to contain. (Actually, the IMF may have been painting too rosy a picture.)

Exercise 7.1 Money demand and money supply

In both cases the money demand function shifts to the right and thus R increases. Note that the relationship between larger Y and higher R is exactly the relationship portrayed by the LM curve (Diagram 7.3).

Exercise 7.2 The LM curve

At point X precautionary demand and speculative demand are comparable to point A (which is an equilibrium because A is on the LM curve), but transaction demand is larger than the equilibrium value (because Y is larger in X than in A). This implies excess demand for money and thus the interst rate will increase. This is a movement towards the LM curve. The equilibrium is stable.

$j \downarrow 0$: This means that speculative demand becomes less interest rate sensitive, for example when the quantity theory of money applies as discussed in Chapter 9.
$j \rightarrow \infty$: Speculative demand is very sensitive to interest rate changes. Lower costs of moving in and out of bonds could enhance j. This is also the case in the liquidity trap discussed in Chapter 9.
$k \downarrow 0$: This means that less money is needed in relation to GPP. General use of debit cards and other innovations (for example, payments by mobile phone) could drive k down.
$k \rightarrow 1$: This means that increasing amounts of money are needed to finance GPP. Hyperinflation, distrust in the health of the banking system or an increase in illegal activities and tax avoidance would enlarge k.

The LM curve is: $R = \dfrac{k}{j} Y + \dfrac{l_{po} - \dfrac{M_0}{P_0}}{j}$

An increase in j shifts the curve downward and makes it flatter.
An increase in k makes the curve steeper.
An increase in P_0 shifts the curve up.
An increase in l_{po} shifts the curve up.
An increase in M_0 shifts the curve down.

Exercise 7.3 Shifting the LM curve

The quadrant shows that the real money supply equals the sum of speculative demand, transaction demand and precautionary demand.

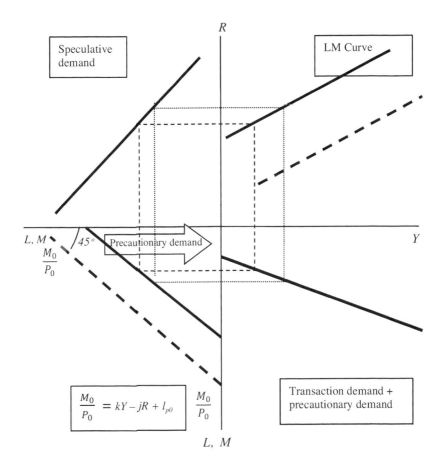

$$\boxed{\frac{M_0}{P_0} = kY - jR + l_{p0}}$$

Exercise 7.4 Monetary policy stance in the Great Recession

Low rate: high speculative demand.

$\frac{M_0}{P_0} = kY + l_{p0}$ so that $Y = \dfrac{\frac{M_0}{P_0} - l_{p0}}{k}$; multiplier is $1/k$.

Exercise 8.1 Excess money supply

The interest rate in a point above LM (for example above E in Diagram 8.2) has too high an interest rate so that speculative demand is reduced below the equilibrium level. Transaction demand is determined by Y. Total money demand is thus lower than the amount that would bring equality between supply and demand.

Exercise 8.2 Reduced form equations in the ISLM model

- Use $I + G = S + T$ so set $I_0 - iR + G_0 = (1 - c) Y - C_0 - cT_0$. Derive R from the money market so that

$$I_0 - i(\frac{k}{j} Y + \frac{l_{po} - \frac{M_0}{P_0}}{j}.) + G_0 = (1 - c) Y - C_0 - cT_0 \text{ which gives the}$$

reduced form equation..

- Use $L = M$. Start with $\frac{M_0}{P_0} = kY - jR + l_{po}$ and derive R from the product

market so that $\frac{M_0}{P_0} = kY - j(\frac{C_0 + I_0 + G_0 - cT_0}{i} - - \frac{(1-c)}{i} Y) + l_{po}$ which gives the

reduced form equation.

- Use $Y = C + I + G$ and derive R from the money market.

Exercise 8.3 Eartheconomic demand

The eartheconomic demand function reflects equilibrium on both the money and the product market and Y is determined by the intersection of the IS and the LM curve. A shift in the exogenous parameters and variables that build the IS curve changes the equilibrium moving Y and thus shifting the eartheconomic demand curve in the same direction. The same is true for the LM curve, but with one exception. A change in the price level shifts the LM curve but *not* the eartheconomic demand curve, where a change in the price level leads to a movement *on* the curve, not *of* the curve.

Exercise 8.4 Eartheconomic demand and the Great Recession

In equation (8.14) an increase in l_{po} and a decrease in C_0 and I_0 reduces the equilibrium value of Y at all price levels P.

Exercise 8.5 Shifting curves

Point E_F results from a fiscal impulse so that Y increases and the increase in eartheconomic demand will *ceteris paribus* increase the interest rate. Point E_M results from a monetary impulse so that R decreases and this leads to an increase of Y via larger I. Since the exercise starts in the same point (E_I) and the movements of R are in opposite directions E_F must represent a higher interest rate than E_M.

Exercise 8.6 Labour market

At a wage higher than W/P^E labour supply exceeds labour demand and drives down the wage. At a wage lower than W/P^E labour demand exceeds labour supply and drives up the wage. The equilibrium is stable.

Labour demand shifts up (increases) if the rental costs of capital increase. Since this is a classical model eartheconomic demand is irrelevant.

Labour supply shifts up (increases) if the population increases, when people value their free time less (this includes cuts in social security) and when labour participation increases (for example, when groups of the population that were previously excluded are allowed to work; this can be a gender issue but also an increase in the age of retirement).

Exercise 8.7 Okun's Law

Note from Figure 8.2 that an increase by 1% on the horizontal axis (unemployment) matches a 3% increase in output gap. β is thus about 3.

Exercise 8.8 Eartheconomic demand and supply

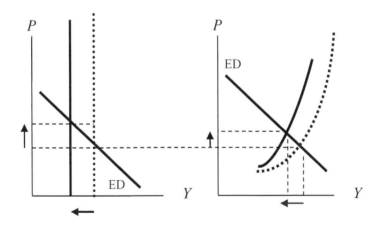

Exercise 9.1 Interest rate sensitivity and the IS curve

A small change in R generates a very strong change in Y.
Fiscal policy is ineffective; monetary policy is very effective.

Exercise 9.2 Interest rate sensitivity and the IS curve

If the components of the IS curve are less interest rate sensitive then you need a larger reduction of R to get the same increase in Y.

Since $Y_s > Y_i$ transaction demand is larger in (Y_s, R_s) and because $R_i < R_s$ speculative demand is larger.

Exercise 9.3 Liquidity trap

Check with Exercises 6.2 and 6.4 for the factors that shift the IS curve outwards.

The liquidity trap is represented by IS_1. Diagram 9.4 shows that the outward shifting LM curve does not result in lower R for IS_1. Only a shift in the IS curve can influence Y under these conditions.

Exercise 9.4 ISLM and full employment

The shift of the IS curve moves the economy from a situation of unemployment towards the full employment level reducing slack in the economy. This acts as an incentive for firms to increase prices (but to a lesser extent than in the left-hand panel of Diagram 9.6). Consequently, the LM curve shifts up (again to a lesser extent) since the real money supply decreases.

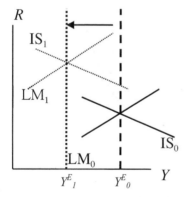

Since the economy starts at full employment the neoclassical analysis is relevant.

Exercise 9.5 Price rigidity

Horizontal part: no price increase. Increasing segment and vertical segment: price increase, but largest price increase occurs in the vertical segment.

Exercise 9.6 Identification

This occurs with a vertical LM curve and an outward shifting IS curve, a vertical IS curve and an upward shifting LM curve and when demand increases at full employment.

Exercise 10.1 Growth in the 1980s to 2000s

Real GPP growth rates 1980 – 2008, according to two sources

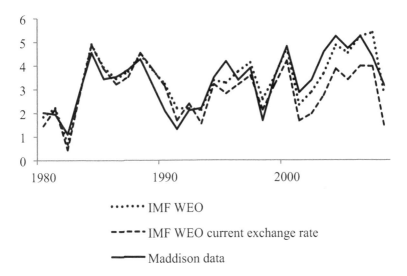

······· IMF WEO

----- IMF WEO current exchange rate

——— Maddison data

The figure shows agreement in the 1980s, a difference of opinion in 1995 and divergence in the 2000s. The data agree on the clear growth slow down, but differ on the extent of the slow-down. The differences for the current exchange rate series reflect changes in the external value of the dollar.

Exercise 10.2 Harrod-Domar model

An increase in the saving rate increases the growth rate of GPP (see equation 10.3). In the Keynesian model this reduces the rate of consumption and hence the multiplier and this leads to lower GPP.

Exercise 10.3 Solow production function

Technology, innovation, efficiency, better education.

Exercise 10.4 Solow model

- Use a ruler to see that the consumption rate is 22mm/32mm (0.9"/1.3") or about 0.7 (but you can also say that it is $1 - s$).
- An increase in the consumption rate shifts down the saving function so that the new equilibrium will be to the left of k_A and at a lower level of productivity than q_A. Production decreases.
- In the Keynesian model an increase in the consumption rate increases the multiplier and thus the equilibrium income level.

Exercise 10.5 Rate of growth

The before and after growth rates are (a) identical and (b) lower than during the transitory phase.

Exercise 10.6 Solow residual

In 1995: 59% and in 2006: 55%.
Manufacturing is more capital intensive.

Exercise 10.7 Growth accounting 1995 – 2005

Growth rate K is 2.9% p.a. and growth rate L is 1.7% p.a.. Total Factor Productivity is $3.8\% - 2.1\% = 1.7\%$.
This is larger (both absolutely and relatively) than in 1965 – 1992.

Exercise 11.1 Poverty trap

For k_A you can refer to the discussion of Diagram 10.2 in the previous chapter; this is now a locally stable equilibrium.

For k_B we have again equality $sq = (n+d)k$, but this time the equilibrium is unstable. In a point to the left of k_A we would have that sq is less than $(n+d)k$ so there $\Delta k < 0$ so the economy falls back to k_A. We would see capital 'shallowing', decreasing the capital-labour ratio and leading to a movement along the production function towards k_A. The opposite happens in points to the right of A so we have a continuous process of capital deepening and productivity growth for larger A. A is a locally unstable equilibrium.

Exercise 11.2 Higher saving provides an escape from the poverty trap

Once the economy has passed the original right hand side equilibrium (so that $k > k_B$ in Diagram 11.1) the economy is out of the poverty trap and the saving rate can return to its original level.

Exercise 11.3 Depreciation and the poverty trap

The analysis of lower d is numerically identical to a reduction in n. However, to reduce d one will have to invest time and money in maintenance and these costs are not reflected in the model.

Exercise 11.4 Mark-up

The mark-up is A/B

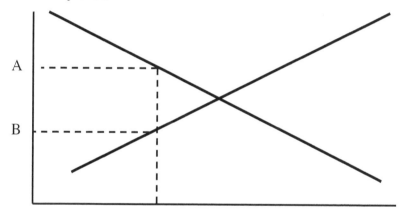

Exercise 11.5 Structural reform

No, supply is insufficient (see the left-hand curve in bottom panel).
The impact on the wage rate is also ambiguous depending on labour demand. On the one hand we can have $W/P(L_A) > W/P(L_0)$, but on the other hand we can have $W/P(L_B) < W/P(L_0)$.

Exercise 12.1 Exponential growth

The halving occurs in 20 years. The annual rate of decay is $70/20 = 3.5\%$ p.a.

Exercise 13.1 Globalization

Text 1 is from J.M. Keynes, *The Economic Consequences of the Peace*, published in 1919. Text 2 is from K. Marx and F. Engels, *Manifesto of the Communist Party*, published in 1848.

Exercise 13.2 Fragmentation

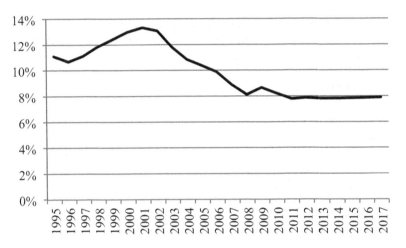

The Figure shows the Herfindahl index. The value in 2008 (about 8%) confirms to the observation reported in Figure 13.4. For 2000 a substantial difference exists (14% *versus* 8%). The difference can be due to the fact that different sources are used. The IMF World Economic Outlook database is in current prices and exchange rates. Maddison's historical series (the source for Figure 13.4) is in constant prices and constant exchange rates.

Exercise 14.1 Comparing fragmentation

In Figure 13.4 (2008, based on Maddison's historical data) the Herfindahl index is 8% and the C3 ratio is 43%. In Figure 14.1 (2010, based on the data of Fouré et al.) the Herfindahl index is 16% and the C3 ratio is 63%. The differences can be explained by the fact that the EU27 are now treated as one state, by the use of different sources and by the fact that the years for which the data are reported refer to different years.

Internet Resources

Since 2010 the availability of data sources on the Earth economy has substantially expanded and many resources are regularly being added. This appendix lists Internet resources that provide a truly global picture. Some of the resources are still in the early phase of development. Often these websites also provide advanced data map facilities.

Central Bank News, *Global Monetary Policy Rate Index*, available at: http://www.centralbanknews.info/p/interest-rates.html.

CPB Netherlands Bureau For Economic Analysis, *Global Industrial Production Excluding Construction* (reported in a separate excel sheet with label: InPro in the CPB World Trade Monitor), available at http://www.cpb.nl/en/world-trade-monitor.

Earth Observation Group of the National Oceanic and Atmospheric Administration, *US Department of Commerce*: *A Global Poverty Map Derived from Satellite Data,* available at: http://www.ngdc.noaa.gov/dmsp/download_poverty.html.

Economist, *The Global Debt Clock,* available at: http://www.economist.com/content/global_debt_clock.

Fraser Institute, *Economic Freedom of the World Index,* available at: http://www.freetheworld.com/reports.html.

International Labour Organization, *Key Indicators of the Labour Market*, (you need to install the program after which the KILM software will run; choose 'world and regional aggregates'), available at: http://kilm.ilo.org/2011/Installation/Application/kilm7install.htm.

International Monetary Fund, *World Economic Outlook Database*, available at http://www.imf.org/external/ns/cs.aspx?id=28.

KOF Swiss Economic Institute, *KOF Index of Globalization*, available at: http://globalization.kof.ethz.ch/

Maddison, A., *Statistics on World Population, GDP and Per Capita GDP, 1-2008 AD 'Maddison's historical series'*, available at the website of the Groningen Growth and Development Centre www.ggdc.net.

United Nations, *UN National Accounts Main Aggregates Database,* available at: http://unstats.un.org/unsd/snaama/

United Nations, *World Population Prospects*, available at:
    http://esa.un.org/unpd/wpp/.
World Bank, *DataBank* [BETA] (choose: 'region world'), available at:
    http://databank.worldbank.org/data/home.aspx.
World Mapper, *Cartograms with Economic and Social Information*, available
    at: http://www.sasi.group.shef.ac.uk/worldmapper/index.html.

At www.eartheconomics.info, you can check for new and additional Internet resources.

References

Atisophon, V., J. Bueren, G. De Paepe, C. Garroway and J.-P. Stijns, 2011, "Revisiting MDG cost estimates from a domestic resource mobilisation perspective", *OECD Development Centre Working Paper 306*, OECD: Paris.

Atkinson, A.B., T. Piketty and E. Saez, 2011, 'Top incomes in the long run of history', *Journal of Economic Literature* **49** (1), pp. 2 – 71.

Banerji, A, A.P. Layton and L. Achuthan, 2012, 'Dating the "world business cycle"', *Applied Economics* **44** (16), pp. 2051 – 63.

Bénassy-Quéré, A. and J. Pisani-Ferry, 2012, 'What international monetary system for a fast-changing world economy?', *CEPII Documents de Travail 2012–04b*, CEPII: Paris.

Bergeijk, P.A.G. van, 1998, 'Did real world per capita income really grow faster in 1870 – 1913 than in 1973 – 1992?', *De Economist* **146**, pp. 143 – 170.

Bergeijk, P.A.G. van, 2009, *Economic Diplomacy and the Geography of International Trade*, Edward Elgar: Cheltenham.

Bos, F., 2009, *The National Accounts as a Tool for Analysis and Policy; In View of History, Economic Theory and Data Compilation Issues*, Verlag Dr Müller: Saarbrücken.

Boulding, K.E., 1966, 'The economics of the coming spaceship earth' in: H. Jarrett (ed.), *Environmental Quality in a Growing Economy*, Johns Hopkins University Press: Baltimore, MD, pp. 3 – 14, available at: http://arachnid.biosci.utexas.edu/courses/THOC/Readings/Boulding_Sp aceshipEarth.pdf.

Chenery, H.B. and A.M. Strout, 1966, "Foreign Assistance and Economic Development," *American Economic Review* **56** (4), pp. 679 – 733.

Colander, D., 2004, 'The strange persistence of the IS/LM model', *Annual Supplement to History of Political Economy* **36**, pp. 305 – 322.

Daly, H.E., 1992, 'From empty-world economics to full-world economics: recognizing an historical turning point in economic development', in: R. Goodland, H.E. Daly and S. El Serafy (eds), *The Transition to Sustainability*, IBRD and Unesco, pp. 23 – 36.

Dreher, A., 2006, 'Does globalization affect growth? Evidence from a new index of globalization', *Applied Economics* **38** (10), pp. 1091 – 1110, updated in: A. Dreher, N. Gaston and P. Martens (2008), *Measuring Globalisation – Gauging its Consequences*, Springer: New York.

Elgin, C. and O. Oztunali, 2012, 'Shadow economies around the world: Model based estimates', Mimeo, Bogazici University, available at: http://www.econ.boun.edu.tr/public_html/RePEc/pdf/201205.pdf.

Elvidge, C.D., P.S. Sutton, K.E. Baugh, B.T. Tuttle, A.T. Howard, E.H. Erwin, B. Bhaduri, and E. Bright, 2009, 'A global poverty map derived from satellite data', *Computers and Geosciences* **35** (8), pp. 1652 – 1660.

Erumban, A.A., B. Los, R. Stherer, M. Timmer and G. de Vries, 2011, 'Slicing up global value chains: The role of China', Mimeo, University of Groningen: Groningen.

Fialho, D., 2012 'Altruism but not quite: the genesis of the Least Developed Country (LDC) category', *Third World Quarterly* **33** (5), pp. 751 – 768.

Fouré, J., A. Bénassy-Quéré and L. Fontagne, 2012, 'The Great Shift: Macroeconomic projections for the world economy at the 2050 horizon', *CEPII Documents de Travail 2012–03*, CEPII: Paris.

Go, D.S. and J. Quijada, 2011, 'Assessing the odds of achieving the MDGs', *Policy Research Working Paper 5825*, World Bank: Washington D.C.

Gosh, J., 2011, 'Re-orienting development in uncertain times', in P.A.G. van Bergeijk, R. van der Hoeven and A. de Haan (eds), *The Financial Crisis and Developing Countries: A Global Multidisciplinary Perspective*, Edward Elgar: Cheltenham, pp. 19 – 36.

Heston, A., R. Summers and B. Aten, 2002, 'Penn World Table Version 6.1, Center for International Comparisons of Production, Income and Prices at the University of Pennsylvania October 2002', available at: http://pwt.econ.upenn.edu/php_site/pwt_index.php

Hickman, J., 2008, 'Problems of interplanetary and interstellar trade', *Astropolitics: The International Journal of Space Politics & Policy* **6** (1), pp. 95 – 104.

Hoeven, R. van der, 2012, 'MDGs post 2015: Beacons in turbulent times or false lights? A contribution to the discussion on a post 2015 Framework for Development', Working paper for the UN System Task team on the post 2015 UN Development Agenda and available at: http://www.un.org/en/development/desa/policy/untaskteam_undf/rolph_van_der_hoeven.pdf.

ICN (International Competition Network), 2005, *Assessing Technical Assistance: Examining the Foundations of Successful Assistance*, Competition Policy Implementation Working Group, Bonn.

ILO (International Labour Organization), 2012a, *Key indicators of the labour market*, 7th Edition, available at: http://kilm.ilo.org.

ILO (International Labour Organization), 2012b, *World of Work Report 2012 Better jobs for a better economy*, ILO: Geneva.

IMF (International Monetary Fund), 2006, *World Economic Outlook: Globalization and Inflation*, April 2006, IMF: Washington DC.

IMF (International Monetary Fund), 2012, *World Economic Outlook: Growth Resuming, Dangers Remain*, April 2012, IMF: Washington DC.

Izurieta, A., 2009, 'Robert Wade on the global financial crisis', *Development and Change* **40** (6), pp. 1153 – 1190.

Kahneman, D., 2011, *Thinking, Fast and Slow*, Farrar Straus & Giroux: New York.

Kaul, I., P. Conceição, K. le Goulven and R.U. Mendoza (eds), 2003, *Providing Global Public Goods: Managing Globalization*, Oxford University Press, New York.

Keynes, J.M., 1984, *The Economic Consequences of the Peace*, Collected Writings II, London: Macmillan (First published in 1919).

Keynes, J.M., 1986, *The General Theory of Employment, Interest and Money*, Collected Writings VII, London: Macmillan (First published in 1936).

Kindleberger, C.P., 1981, 'Dominance and leadership in the international economy', *International Studies Quarterly* **25** (2), pp. 242 – 254.

Kindleberger, C.P., 1986, 'International public goods without international government', *American Economic Review* **76** (1), pp. 1 – 13.

King, R.G., 2000, 'The new IS-LM model: language, logic, and limits', *Federal Reserve Bank of Richmond Economic Quarterly* **86** (3), pp. 45 – 103.

Kondratieff, N.D., 1935, 'The long waves in economic life', *The Review of Economics and Statistics* **17** (6), pp. 105 – 115.

Korotayev, A. V. and S.V Tsirel, 2010, 'A spectral analysis of world GDP dynamics: Kondratieff waves, Kuznets swings, Juglar and Kitchin cycles in global economic development, and the 2008 – 2009 economic crisis', *Structure and Dynamics* **4** (1), available at: http://www.escholarship.org/uc/item/9jv108xp#page-1.

Krugman, P., 1978, 'The theory of interstellar trade', formally published in: *Economic Inquiry* (2010) **48**, pp. 1119 – 1123, and available at: http://www.princeton.edu/~pkrugman/interstellar.pdf.

Kuhn, T.S., 1972, *The Structure of Scientific Revolutions*, 2nd enlarged edition, International Encyclopedia of United Science, **2** (2), University of Chicago Press: Chicago.

Kumar, S. and R.R. Russell, 2002, 'Technological change, technological catch-up, and capital deepening: relative contributions to growth and convergence', *American Economic Review* **92** (3), pp. 527 – 548.

Lequiller, F. and D. Blades, 2006, *Understanding National Accounts*, OECD: Paris.

Lin, J.F. and D. Rosenblatt, 2012, 'Shifting patterns of economic growth and rethinking development', *WPS 6040*, World Bank: New York.

Maddison, A., 1995, *Monitoring the World Economy 1820–1992*, OECD: Paris.

Mankiw, N.G., 2008, *Principles of Economics*, South-Western: Mason, OH.

Mankiw, N.G., D. Romer and D. Weil, 1992, 'A contribution to the empirics of economic growth', *Quarterly Journal of Economics* **107**, pp. 407 – 437.

Marshall, M.G. and B.R. Cole, 2011, *Global Report 2011: Conflict, Governance, and State Fragility*, Center for Systemic Peace: Vienna, VA.

Marx, K. and F. Engels, 1848, Manifesto of the communist party, available at: http://www.anu.edu.au/polsci/marx/classics/manifesto.html.

Meadows, D.H., D.L. Meadows, J. Randers, W. W. Behrens III, 1972, *The Limits to Growth: A Report to The Club of Rome,* Universe Books: New York.

Milanovich, B., 2009, 'Global inequality and the global inequality extraction ratio: The story of the past two centuries', *Policy Research Working Paper 5044*, World Bank: Washington DC.

Morgenstern, O., 1950, *On the Accuracy of Economic Observations*, Princeton University Press: Princeton.

Okun, A.M., 1962, 'Potential GNP, its measurement and significance', *Cowles Foundation Paper 190*, Yale University: New Haven, available at http://cowles.econ.yale.edu/P/cp/p01b/p0190.pdf.

Olson, M., 1965, *The Logic of Collective Action: Public Goods and the Theory of Groups*, Harvard University Press: Harvard.

Olson, M., 1982, *The Rise and Decline of Nations: Economic Growth, Stagflation, and Social Rigidities*, Yale University Press: New Haven.

Ortiz, I. and M. Cummins, 2011, 'Global inequality: Beyond the bottom billion: A rapid review of income distribution in 141 countries', *UNICEF Social and Economic Policy Working Paper*, UNICEF: New York.

Papenhausen, C., 2008, 'Causal mechanisms of long waves', *Futures* **40** (9), pp. 788 – 79.

Rodrik, D., 2000, 'How far will international economic integration go?', *Journal of Economic Perspectives* **14** (1), pp. 177 – 86.

Sachs, J.D. and F. Larrain B., 1993, *Macroeconomics in the Global Economy*, Harvester Wheatsheaf: New York, etc.

Sali-I-Martin, X., 2002, 'The world distribution of income (estimated from individual country distributions', *NBER Working Paper 8933,* NBER: Cambridge, MA.

Sandler, T., 1998, 'Global and regional public goods: a prognosis for collective action', *Fiscal Studies* **19** (3), pp. 221 – 247.

Schumpeter, J.A., 1954, *The History of Economic Analysis,* Allen & Unwin: London.

Smith, A., 1976, *An Inquiry into the Nature and Causes of the Wealth of Nations*, Canna's edition, Claredon Press: Oxford (First published in 1776).

Solow, R.M., 1956, 'A contribution to the theory of economic growth', *Quarterly Journal of Economics* **70** (1), pp. 65–94.

Solow, R.M., 1957, 'Technical change and the aggregate production function', *Review of Economics and Statistics* **39** (3), pp. 312 – 20.

Stern, N., 2006, *The Economics of Climate Change: The Stern Review*, Cambridge University Press: Cambridge.

Taleb, N.N., 2007, *The Black Swan; The impact of the highly improbable*, Penguin: London.

Turrini, A., W. Roeger and I. Pal Székely, 2012, 'Banking crises, output loss, and fiscal policy', *CESifo Economic Studies* **58** (1), pp. 181 – 219.

United Nations, 2003, *National Accounts: A Practical Introduction*, New York; http://unstats.un.org/unsd/publication/SeriesF/seriesF_85.pdf.

United Nations, 2011, *World Population Prospects: The 2010 Revision*, UN: New York.

United Nations, 2012, *Inclusive Wealth Report 2012: Measuring Progress Toward Sustainability*, Cambridge University Press: Cambridge.

World Bank, 2010, *The MDGs after the Crisis, Global Monitoring Report 2010,* World Bank: Washington, DC.

World Bank, 2011a, *Global Development Horizons 2011: Multipolarity - The New Global Economy*, World Bank: Washington, DC.

World Bank 2011b, *The Changing Wealth of Nations: Measuring Sustainable Development in the New Millennium*, World Bank: Washington, DC

Index